Dearest Katie,

Thank you for being my

"Earth Angel"

A light that has led me to be

Now Here I

Blessings

Peace &

# Surrounded by Angels

by

## Angela Amoroso

iUniverse, Inc.
New York   Bloomington

*Surrounded by Angels*

*iUniverse books may be ordered through booksellers or by contacting:*

*iUniverse*
*1663 Liberty Drive*
*Bloomington, IN 47403*
*www.iuniverse.com*
*1-800-Authors (1-800-288-4677)*

*ISBN: 978-0-595-48779-0 (pbk)*
*ISBN: 978-0-595-48833-9 (cloth)*
*ISBN: 978-0-595-60841-6 (ebk)*

*Printed in the United States of America*

# Table of Contents

# About Angela and Drew

Angela Amoroso and her husband, Drew Skinner, lost their infant daughter, Isabella, to Sudden Infant Death Syndrome (SIDS) in December of 2004. Isabella died in Angela's arms with Drew sitting right next to her. They know firsthand that SIDS is painless and babies do not suffer.

Angela is no stranger to the grieving community. Her best friend from high school passed away suddenly at age nineteen from a congenital heart defect. Angela's only sibling, a sister, passed from an inoperable, malignant brain tumor. Her father passed suddenly from heart disease complicated by diabetes, and her mother suffered from Alzheimer's for almost twenty years. These life experiences that brought forth miraculous "coincidences" inspired Angela to write this book. Surrounded by Angels, and the accompanying CD of original songs written by both her and her husband are available on their Web site at www. IsabellasGiraffeClub.org.

Isabella's passing was a deep calling for Angela and Drew to help others move through their grief. Using their personal creative talents and professional expertise in the performing arts and music, they created a presentation of their experiences and wrote original songs to compliment each presentation.

They shared this artistic memorial tribute at the International SIDS/Still Birth Conference in Washington DC in September of 2005. Angela and Drew have been involved with many educational programs, including speaking at various medical seminars and symposiums and presenting at training sessions to emergency workers, first responders, and public health nurses and doctors. They are part of the Southern California Regional SIDS Council that reports to the Governor. They have served on the 2006 and 2008 California State SIDS Conference Planning Committee.

Inspired by their tiny daughter, they founded Isabella's Giraffe Club just two days after she was born. Their fundraising efforts since Isabella's passing at the time of this printing include $55,000 to the University of California San Diego Medical Center, Infant Special Care Center.

Angela and Drew wish to share their message of a deep knowing that love never dies, it merely changes form. And for them, this just may be the meaning behind their miraculous photographs.

*"Isabella's Kiss" September 2005*
*Photo by Carla Pettit*

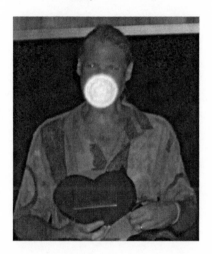

*In the oneness of love, we dedicate this book in gratitude for the journey and every precious soul who we have met along the way.*

*Thank you for the clarity!*
*And Above All …*
*The Good Vibrations!*

*In Love and Light*
*Angela and Drew*

# Introduction -

## NowHere

*"When we are motivated by goals that have deep meaning, by dreams that need completion, by pure love that needs expressing, then we truly live."*

—*Greg Anderson*

August of 2004, I was lying flat on my back staring at the ceiling in my hospital room, wondering how I got there. There was no apparent medical reason for my water to break so unexpectedly. My pregnancy at only twenty-four weeks gestation was coming to a rapid end—our baby girl hung on inside. My husband and I were introduced to a compassionate neonatologist whose job it was to explain the dim, seemingly hopeless resuscitation methods if our daughter was to be born within the next seventy-two hours.

We had a lot to think about. Up until that moment we had been contemplating all of the organic ways to give birth in a natural environment. We had romanticized about having a gentle birth with music and laughter. It was our responsibility and our joy to provide our baby with the best start in life. Now I felt like a failure, desperate and frightened that these amazing new technologies were our only hope for our baby to survive at all. Yet, these new technologies still needed my help to keep her on the inside for as long as possible. My organic nature instantly grew a new respect for the medical community. We had to try and buy more time, together. I accepted the challenge and my role as "mommy" took on another dimension.

The doctors kept us carefully monitored, recording every heartbeat and every ounce of liquid that was replenishing itself in my leaking womb. It was my job to keep my body still, yet my mind raced in wonder of how medical science had come so far in my lifetime. We were preparing to witness a real miracle, assisted by modern science. For my husband and me, we entered a world that was surreal. Even more unbelievable was the team of miracle workers: an endless stream of doctors, nurses, and technicians who harmonized in this great scientific orchestra to bring forth life. They participated in miracles every day; it was their job.

I began to have a new relationship with the child inside me. She no longer felt like a baby but a grown-up, human soul awaiting its birth. I began to have conversations with this angelic being. The conversations were simple at first—mental coaching for her to remain inside, no matter how good the outside might have looked, from whatever her perspective might have been. Then the conversations changed to my deepest thoughts and fears regarding the world as I see it. I found myself apologizing for the human condition that I was birthing her into. I began to explore what I thought could be the origin of the problems facing humanity.

Technology had blasted us into the twenty-first century, connecting us to the World Wide Web. There, a global awareness, having the capacity to see into every corner of our planet, still left the human heart adrift. War, famine, and disease not only still existed but were thriving despite our depleted resources. How could I explain that our holy books and their philosophies had barely changed in five thousand years, and so our ability to "stay awake" and create a world that works for everyone sustains an illusion that makes it seem too hard.

I call it the "Post It" syndrome. I direct a small children's theater in an above-average neighborhood. We have a seating capacity of eighty people. One day, a mom came in early before the performance and, without asking, began writing "reserved" on little yellow Post-It notes. She then began sticking one on each of the fifteen front-row seats. I guess it never occurred to her that the other nineteen families, who later were going to be patiently waiting in line outside, deserved the same front row as she did. When I told her she would have to stop, her response was not, "Oops, I'm sorry," but angry and defensive. I wondered why it was possible for her to think that she was more important. If that's how it looks in the most benign of circumstances, how can we expect countries with political and religious dichotomies to get along? In a world that works for everyone, perhaps we need to evolve our spiritual understanding to keep up with the advancement of technology.

Despite the bleak outlook portrayed in our everyday media, I have always thought that there is more beauty to be found in the precious present than most people are willing to see. Cynical friends often accuse me of wearing rose-colored glasses. My dad taught me that you can get more bees with honey! His lessons taught me to be cheerful, especially in the eye of a storm.

I wanted with all my heart to have the opportunity to show my baby girl that life is beautiful. In my mind I took her on a magic carpet ride. I imagined hiking with my precious child through sandy trails, blanketed in pine needles, their mountain fragrance baking in the hot summer breeze. We soared over oceans with our hair blowing and sun-kissed by salty wet air. I saw her take her first step and ride bikes with her big sisters. I saw her sitting on top of her Daddy's shoulders, so high up in the sky. And then I saw her dance. Oh, how she twirled and whirled in her snowflake costume. In wonder and awe I heard her giggle, and I knew that together we would create our wildest dreams to come true.

# Chapter One -
# Isabella, Dedicated to God

*"O welcome pure-eyed Faith, white-handed Hope, Thou hovering angel, girt with golden wings!"*
                                                        —*John Milton "Comus"*

How do I begin to tell the story about a real live Angel? It is a story about a life filled with miracles and love. It is the witnessing of a great soul whose command post was from a tiny little body. This is a soul who continues to challenge us to be the best that we can be, a soul whose story will captivate your attention and compel your heart to expand. It is the revealing of the magnitude of friendships and family in their darkest hour. It is a story about healing, a process that is always working. It is a demonstration of the ever-expanding human spirit.

I will try to paint you a picture that only my heart knows how to tell. Where will I find the words? I will begin with my dream to give birth, never imagining that it would be to such a child. My husband, Drew, named her Isabella, which means dedicated to God.

I always dreamed of having another child. My first daughter is a beautiful gift who entered my life in my youth. She is now 27. Her life is an enfoldment of beauty and grace. Her father and I divorced when she was still an infant. She and I grew up together. She was my daughter, my best friend, and even my business partner. I adored her and wanted to inspire her to reach for the stars and follow her dreams.

My parenting during her teens was not as graceful as I would have liked it to be. If only teenagers came with directions! The young adult who I raised in my youth is still my pride and joy. She continues to create her life to be a balance of service and gratitude, and she shows up with a smile and a song that brings more joy wherever she goes. During her last years in high school, I had made some unfortunate choices, and by the time she was twenty-one years old, I was rebuilding my life, working sixteen-hour days and trying to find a way to put the past behind me. I was clearly in a new chapter of my life. As I passed the big 4-0, the dream for another child was fading, but I never lost hope that someday I would find true love.

During the summer of 2003, I participated in a compassionate communication class. The facilitator used animal puppets to represent different styles of communication. He chose the giraffe to be the compassionate communicator because they are the mammals with the biggest hearts, not surprising when you think about how powerful the heart muscle must be to pump the blood up the long and graceful necks of these giants.

Days later, a friend set up a blind date for me and a handsome, gentle giant measuring six feet, eight inches tall. Our casual first meeting was camouflaged by his willingness to deliver a donated set of mirrors to my dance studio. As his giant frame graced the doorway, his smile warmed my heart. He left with my phone number, and a week later we had our first date, never to be apart again. Forty-one years of hoping, wishing, and waiting—this was finally it! My true love, my very own giraffe named Drew, and the kindest man I had ever met.

We were married by the Reverend Christian Sorensen, on my birthday on top of a carpet of pine needles under majestic towering trees overlooking the ocean. Our marriage is the most amazing birthday gift that I have ever received. Since then, we never exchange presents on our day, merely experiences. My husband has two gorgeous daughters from a previous marriage. They are incredibly talented and independent young women. He was divorced from their mother when they were just two and three years old. Raising these precious young ladies as a single dad was not easy.

Drew found refuge at the local dance studio and soon called himself a "ballet dad." His regular appearance every weekend, taking his daughters to class, gave the directors the idea to launch Drew in his own ballet career. For the next nine years, in full costume and makeup, he played "Mother Ginger" in their annual Nutcracker production. Confident and complete as a father, he had not planned on having more children at his age, yet his love for me was more than indulgent.

My body clock was ticking, so we wasted no time and soon told the world that we were having what else but a baby giraffe! I imagined our child to be just like its daddy, tall and loving, so "baby giraffe" seemed appropriate. A local children's store that spring coincidentally had a complete line of baby giraffe clothing. My girlfriend Katy indulged me and bought every outfit, towel, blanket—you name it—that had giraffes printed on it. My girlfriends even gave me a baby shower and decorated the nursery with nothing but giraffes. Our world became very orange.

We were shopping for a new house to fit our expanding family. My husband was dreaming of a cabin. I was dreaming of the ocean. The perfect home in our price range miraculously became available in a seller's market that had soared beyond reason! There it was, a cabin, surrounded by Torrey Pine trees, complete with ocean views! You could hear the waves crashing at night and check the surf in your pajamas in the morning. In the living room was a wall of floor-to-ceiling windows that left you feeling like a giraffe seeing eye to eye with the treetops. We had no way of knowing that this view was the foreshadowing of what was to come.

We were scheduled to move in late August. Just two days before we were to receive the key for our nest up in the trees, for no apparent reason, while standing at the register in an office supply store, my water began to leak. In a strange calm, I left everything on the counter and told the clerk I'd be back later. I drove myself directly to the nearest emergency room.

When I walked myself into the emergency room, I used a folder to cover my embarrassingly soaked pants. I very calmly told the nurse that I thought my water had broken. In disbelief and with somewhat lighthearted sarcasm she mocked, "Now, why would you think a thing like that?" Even the nurse wanted to believe that it could be something else! I removed my "cover up" and watched the expression in her eyes leap into sheer panic. Within seconds I was sitting in a wheelchair, and suddenly life as I knew it would never be the same again.

I was transferred by ambulance to the best hospital in the region that was renowned for caring for premature babies in critical condition. I had only been pregnant for twenty-four weeks. I called my husband in shock, and asked him to bring my hypnobirthing book to the hospital. I had been told that hypnobirthing was the new rage in natural childbirth.

My first daughter had been born with midwives, but I did not accomplish the calm birth I had intended. The labor pains turned out to be labor cramps, and although I succeeded in bringing my daughter into this world without an aspirin, I thought that I could do better to stay on top of those contractions if I tried another method. I was excited to try something new, and my husband and I had already gone to our first hypnobirthing class. On my bumpy and leaky ambulance ride to the hospital, I was trying to be positive and thinking that we were just going to have life come a little early, so I better start studying. I kept thinking that everything was going to be fine. I had waited more than twenty years to have my dream come true. How could it take such a terrible turn for the worst?

That book was on my bed twenty-four hours into this nightmare when an amazing neonatologist, Dr. Jaime Jones, came to my room for a visit. In tow were two wide-eyed medical students ready to study every move he would make, every word he would utter. His job was to bring us the bad news. It was the talk that detailed the reality of what would happen if our daughter was to be born within the next seventy-two hours. Her chances of survival were bleak. Most babies born at twenty-four weeks are not born breathing. Unimaginable is the color of a lifeless baby that has arrived too many months before its due date.

Medical technology leaves the decision for the parents to choose. Our choices if Isabella came within the next few days were to (a) make some kind of technical, inhuman, heroic effort to bring our baby back to life, or (b) accept fate and experience life and death on what should have been one of the happiest days of our lives. Babies who do survive any one of the various resuscitation methods are faced with the incredible and painful challenge to grow on the outside. This leaves parents seemingly helpless by the bedside, hearts wrenching as they ride an emotional roller coaster watching their womb-less infant's battle for survival. Therefore, every day that we could keep her on the inside counted big time.

They gave me steroids to help her lungs develop more quickly. For my daughter, seventy-two hours more on the inside with the support of the steroids could offer more hope. And every day after that, the chance of survival improves; however, no one really ever mentions the "against all odds" statistics. All Drew and I had was faith the size of a mustard seed. That's the funny thing about faith. No one has more or less, you either have it or you don't, and now in these critical moments we mustered it up!

Together with Dr. Jones, we created a resuscitation plan, putting our faith into his experienced hands. Plan A would be tragic: we would let the doctors determine her condition and ultimately let her go peacefully. Plan B would be in place seventy-two hours later when there would be a better chance that they could save her.

This was no ordinary doctor. I have had a lifetime filled with a myriad of physicians, coast to coast. When I was seventeen, my only sister was diagnosed in Chicago with an inoperable, malignant brain tumor. In New York, our mother suffered from Alzheimer's for almost twenty years, and our dad had lived with a serious heart condition that was complicated by diabetes. Since my sister passed away in the prime of her life, I had the responsibility to take care of our aging parents and make countless medical decisions alone.

I had experienced modern medicine firsthand and chose to practice an organic lifestyle for myself. I don't have a regular doctor, I rarely get a cold, and I see a chiropractor and acupuncturist for those rare occasions when I am a little under the weather.

This time was clearly different. This neonatologist, sitting at the foot of my bed, demonstrated more compassion and respect than any doctor in my considerable past experience. He intuitively seemed to understand who we were and noticed the hypno-book on my bed. He asked with sincere interest if this was something we were doing. We told him yes, and he told us that he had read the book! He shared his positive thoughts on birthing and seemed genuinely pleased that we were the alternative-medicine types.

He stayed with us for almost two and a half hours and left us inspired. Some seventy-two hours later, he peeked his head in my door and like a cheerleader shouted, "Plan B!" We had been successful in keeping our baby on the inside for those first and most critical hours. Now I would be transferred upstairs to stay for as long as possible. Now every day counted! She had a chance! I cried tears of joy.

I moved into the hospital, and my husband moved into our dream cabin. My first daughter, Jeanne Marie, took the night shift and slept in a chair in my hospital room every evening. I was determined to have life go on as usual and decided I had to keep my mind busy and my body still. In my "other world" I had a lot of other little girls counting on me too. There was an all-children's Nutcracker to produce, and you know what they say in showbiz: "The show must go on!"

My husband brought my office to me—laptop, printers, and files. I was planning to be there for the long haul, so the best thing I could do was keep my mind moving forward. I even held production and faculty meetings from my new office.

My girlfriends replaced the hospital meals with daily organic deliveries from the local health food store. I ate like a queen, and most importantly I meditated for two to four hours every day. I went to sleep every night listening to inspirational talks by the Reverend Dr. Michael Beckwith from the AGAPE International Spiritual Center.

Staying calm was imperative. Even my dogs were given permission to visit. I had the best care not only from my nurses and doctors, but from my friends, my family, and my amazing husband. Best of all was the incredible prayer support that seemed to come from everywhere, including hundreds of students and their families who kept us in their good thoughts. It became easy to remain calm and positive for the health of my unborn child. After all, there was no other option.

Remaining in bed for almost two weeks despite this amazing group effort was taking its toll on my morale. I longed to wash my hair and take a shower. Just when I thought I couldn't last another day, my best friend Barbara and her daughter Caitlin flew in from New York on Labor Day weekend for a surprise visit. Their arrival renewed my strength to be strong for the task at hand.

That same Friday night one of my students' moms stopped by with her husband on their way to a ball game, fully outfitted in baseball fan apparel. I was puzzled at how she knew where to find me. With the exception of my staff and close friends, we kept visitors at bay. Apparently, earlier that day she had coincidentally run into one of my girlfriends at the soccer field who had given her my room number. She explained that she actually worked in the hospital in the Neonatal Intensive Care Unit and would be my baby's nurse! Imagine that, after several years of watching her husband and daughter perform in my shows, now my family would be on her stage. The tables had turned. What a beautiful yet strange coincidence that this amazing "Nurse Lynn" would show up at such a critical time in our lives with a new part to play.

Labor Day has always been one of my favorite holidays. I love to just relax on the last long weekend before school starts. The air starts to change, true signs that autumn (my favorite time of year) is on its way. Labor Day has also lent itself to be my own little personal joke. I delivered my first daughter with midwives and was clearly surprised when my "labor pains" turned out to be "labor cramps." No one had ever warned me about this. Pain I was ready for, but cramps? No way! However, she was born six hours later without any medical intervention, and I always looked forward to the day when I would get to do it again.

So, whenever I wish one of my students a happy birthday, I wish their parents a happy "Labor Day." The joke was now on me. It was my turn for a happy Labor Day. Right after midnight on Labor Day morning, Monday, September 6, 2004, my contractions started. I temporarily had to accept my immediate surroundings and enter a sterile operating room. The serene setting that I imagined with a midwife was replaced by a surgical team and bright lights. A spinal block was administered as they prepared to deliver our baby as quickly as possible. The good news was that my husband remained by my side whispering our hypnobirthing techniques to keep my mind on positive thoughts instead of drifting off to ponder a terrifying outcome.

Regardless of my fears, it was show time. The stage was set, the cast present. It had been thirteen days of motionless rehearsal, and now on Labor Day, miraculously breathing on her own, weighing in at a whopping one pound and eleven ounces, this beautiful baby girl became the star of the show. The romantic birth that I had anticipated ended in a classical C-section, and the tiny body was whisked away to the arms of Nurse Lynn who had her sleeves rolled up, ready to do what was necessary to keep our baby girl alive. My husband followed the baby, and I stayed behind with my anesthesiologist, trying to stay calm with my hypnobirthing exercises while they sewed me back together.

When my husband found me in the recovery room, he was overjoyed to tell me the story of our tiny dancer, who, with eyes wide open, stretched her neck back in order to make eye contact with her daddy giraffe. It felt as though it was some kind of divine recognition. There he stood watching over her in awe as the medical team worked harmoniously together with seamless precision to acclimate this tiny wonder to her waterless surroundings. There was something different about her from the very start. We were later given a book that shared these words of the second Dalai Lama, Gendun Gyatso Palzangpo (1475–1541), from Tibet: "The child is said to have been born with exceedingly clear eyes and to have greeted everyone present." We were unaware of the actual Angel in our midst.

I didn't get to hold my precious child for days; her skin seemed still sticky to the touch. All I could do was sit and stare at her tininess. I felt she had this beautiful spiritual umbilical cord that allowed her to float in and out of her body that was working so hard to grow big and strong. Then came a day when I absolutely felt that she no longer drifted back and forth but had "settled in."

Isabella, weighing only 755 grams, was far from being out of the woods. The medical professionals started a PIC line that would be inserted near her ankle and work its way up to her chest cavity. This ultra-thin catheter would deliver all the necessary nutrients and medicines. On day two, this feisty gal kicked out her PIC line and, with only my mother's milk being delivered through a tiny tube in her nose, Isabella miraculously gained weight to the amazement of her doctors and nurses. In fact, during the entire ninety-two day hospital stay, she only gained weight, extremely unusual for a preemie.

Isabella received quite the reputation at the hospital for her dislike of wet diapers and meals that were not delivered on time. It did not take long for her team of caregivers to fall in love with her. What we found unusual was this technical jungle, always equipped with tubes and wires, permitted and encouraged us (in between all the tests and X-rays, bells and whistles) to use baby massage, aromatherapy, and even allowed a visit from our chiropractor to administer his particular brand of healing. The neonatologist who was so kind introduced us to a nurse who was going to start a medical study for baby massage. We became the "practice family," forever blessed to be given such an incredible tool to let our baby feel the love and healing touch of her parents amidst all the pain and discomfort of the necessary medical intervention.

You may ask, "How did we find such an incredible medical staff to be so sensitive to our organic parental needs?" Clearly, Isabella—on her own creative mission from heaven—had a higher power working on her behalf to make certain that she had only the best medical care that this beautiful planet has to offer. The teachings of Abraham, translated by Esther and Jerry Hicks, call it the Law of Attraction. We make it a family practice every day to notice a blessing more than any challenge.

We did not experience the roller-coaster ride of ups and downs that are typically expected in this kind of fragile situation. By day three, I was convinced that there must be some other reason why we were here. Clearly our baby was as "healthy" as could be expected under the circumstances. There were no heart, eye, or lung problems. Even though she was born breathing on her own, hospital procedure required her to be intubated. That lasted for only twelve hours after her birth, enough time to convince the doctors that she could be left to breathe on her own with a little assistance from time to time. So why were we here?

# Chapter Two -

# Love Knows No Bounds

*"There was a pause—just long enough for an angel to pass, flying slowly."*

—Ronald Firbank *"Vainglory"*

When I moved to California, I was inspired by my friend Katie Sullivan who taught me about philanthropy. She was my mentor who awakened me to the profound destiny that each one of us has to contribute and give back to our society to the best of our ability.

I had established Super*Kids to be a children's performing arts company dedicated to children's awareness of environmental concerns, world health, peace and community service. I tried to inspire my students to be ready for any situation that needed support through the creative vehicle of the performing arts. Through our performances we had done an impressive job of inspiring children to be local philanthropists. We had raised thousands of dollars that had been generously donated to a variety of worthy organizations. Perhaps this neonatal intensive care center could benefit from our service—finally, a reason for this madness.

We were told that today one in eight babies are born premature, and one-hundred thousand babies in California will have some kind of intensive care experience. Even the March of Dimes has changed their focus to helping preemies. I asked the director of nurses about the needs of this miracle unit because, as soon as we could, we would give back to this amazing facility.

Focusing on the goal instead of the daunting task at hand has always been my gift. For me, a little pinch of denial can be a wonderful thing. I searched the expression on her face that spoke a thousand words, including that it would be wise to wait until after we brought our baby home. I assured her that multi-tasking was my gift and that thinking of others was part of our healing process. I could tell that she did not know where to begin; so much assistance was needed in every area. I interrupted the awkward pause by inquiring about the incubators. "Give me one thing to focus on for starters," I said. It seemed logical for me since my little baby was sleeping in one of these old beds. She walked me over to a state-of-the-art machine. It was fantastic. It was an incubator that was fully equipped so that the baby inside was not moved unnecessarily. Too much stimulation for these tiny humans taken too early from their wombs was not a good thing.

I stood in awe of this technological wonder. It had a long steel pole at the end that allowed the cover to rise up and down like something out of Star Wars. It kept the perfect temperature, had its own scale and offered a plethora of technologies that gave the unimaginable situation ease and grace. "Perfect," I said. "How much is one of these?" She told me that since they are very expensive, they only had two, and that it would be wonderful to have more. Now I had a ball to run with.

Later my husband went on a tour of the NICU. He came back to my room and said with that smile that makes my life complete, "Guess what they call those state-of-the-art incubators, with the long steel neck?"

"What?" I said.

Without hesitation he answered, "The Giraffe, and it's made by General Electric!"

Inspired by the strength that she demonstrated just days after our daughter was born, Isabella's Giraffe Club was launched.

Those around us embraced the idea and got to work so we could focus on growing Isabella. A generous and selfless angel named Linda in San Francisco worked with the company that donated their time and developed the logo. Paul Lorenz created the Web pages that attached to the studio's Web site and worked with the hospital to be able to take donations online that would be directly donated to the NICU. It was divine inspiration in action. We were able to formally announce Isabella's Giraffe Club with a full-page ad in the program for our Nutcracker production. We were on fire with ideas of what Isabella's Giraffe Club could be in the future.

The baby massage study nurse educated us in the value of Kanga Care. It is a concept that was developed from observations done in Bolivia. During the absence of adequate medical care, impoverished women were sent home with their preemies to watch them die. Under the most devastating of circumstances and no hope, these babies survived! The mothers held their babies, skin to skin, twenty-four hours a day.

And so we were at the hospital every day, sometimes twice a day—sometimes until 2 am,, sometimes I arrived at 5 am. We knew we would not be able to keep up this pace and produce the Nutcracker. There were so many other little girls counting on us too. I thought if I invited twenty-four of my girlfriends to administer Kanga Care, we could have Isabella's needs covered twenty-four hours a day. We quickly realized that our enthusiasm was dampened by the reality of her fragile state. The need to limit germs was critical. We limited our "Kanga Moms" to two, Lori and Katy.

They soon became Isabella's "Other Moms" who gave my husband and me time to regenerate our weary hearts from our demanding schedule. There were so many wonderful people who touched our lives and brought forth so much love and support. It fed our determination to move through the seemingly treacherous terrain before us.

Everything was going along so well. We felt like we were home among all the hospital monitors, bells and whistles. Lori and Katy took pictures regularly and decorated the incubator with letters of support and gratitude for the nurses and doctors. They updated them every week to keep the medical team aware of how much this tiny baby meant to a whole community that would welcome her arrival home for Christmas. Katy even made an incubator cover to block out the light so Isabella's new womb was dark and toasty. The fabric was covered in butterflies and dragonflies, snowflakes, giraffes and ballet slippers!

We were halfway there. Isabella was over three pounds and looking more and more like a real baby. Then we received a call late one night that told us to return to the hospital. Our stomachs churned—what could be so wrong? When we arrived, the atmosphere had changed. Suddenly we were in a real NICU with life-threatening matters. The doctors could barely make eye contact with us. Her night nurse looked as if she had been crying.

We looked at our daughter and saw that her tummy was bloated. They had to take her off her regular feeding tube with my milk and had placed her on antibiotics. The X-rays showed bubbles in her intestines; the diagnosis was leaning toward NEC, Necrotizing Enterocolitis, a life-threatening intestinal disease. Only time would tell.

We were devastated and felt that this outcome was one that we could not accept. We needed a miracle. I wondered how we could get the most prayers happening at the same time to make this go away. Then I was inspired. Through my tears I called Kanga Jane, the back-up Kanga Mom, who became known for her faithful prayer work. Her children went to a religious school, so the next day the principal announced Isabella's name over the loud speaker. Simultaneously, several-hundred children bowed their heads in prayer. The following day the X-rays showed that the bubbles were gone. The doctors immediately took her off the antibiotics, and she went back on regular feeds with my milk.

From the look of amazement on the medical team's faces, the only explanation was … a real live miracle.

A few weeks later Thanksgiving arrived. We had so much to be thankful for. Isabella was five pounds and almost ready to come home. Our chiropractor came with us on Thanksgiving morning to give Isabella a treatment. He held her in his arms and chanted a lullaby in Spanish. Completely relaxed with her arms outstretched, she went into a state of bliss that was remarkably serene. A nonstop grin was on her face with her eyes closed. It looked as if she were having a conversation in her mind with either God or Bill Cosby. She was *so* happy. Nurse Lynn stood by in utter amazement and shared that she had never seen a preemie so relaxed and smiling like that for such a long time.

The following week was the Nutcracker production. Everyone was extremely excited for us, knowing that Isabella's homecoming was imminent. In the production I choreographed a unique part for the little three year olds to be baby snowflakes. They stole the show. They entered the stage one at a time to the sounds of a cooing audience, each one demonstrating that no two are alike, just like real snowflakes. The entire weekend enthusiastic families kept saying, "Oh, we bet you can't wait; in just a couple of years Isabella will be on stage as a baby snowflake."

During the nutty Nutcracker season with our demanding parenting schedule, we never missed a rehearsal or a day at the hospital with Isabella. After long evenings at the theater, we went directly to the hospital to see our baby snowflake until the wee hours of the morning. When we left with the sunrise, nurses would warn us that they didn't want to see us again until lunch time.

I managed a quick trip to the store since I wanted to purchase her homecoming outfit myself. And what did I find? You guessed it: a fluffy warm snowflake jumper. The very next day after the Nutcracker was over, on December 6, 2004, exactly three months after she was born, we received the wonderful news … Isabella was free to come home.

I never imagined that leaving the hospital would be so difficult. Suddenly it was as if we were taking her away from home instead of bringing her home. The nurses who I had shared motherhood with said their good-byes; it all felt so strange. These people had become family, and now we were to say our good-byes and have a nice life? That was it?

Nurse Lynn went over all of the emergency procedures, which we had trained so carefully for, one last time. Now Isabella's watch would be ours alone. I felt thrilled and scared, happy and sad all at the same time. It was hard to imagine what life would be like without all of the monitors, bells, whistles, and wires— Isabella unplugged!

Nurse Lynn carried Isabella as we walked slowly out of the NICU and down the halls to the front doors of the hospital with our baby, a trip we had made over a hundred times with empty arms. The final moment came. Nurse Lynn passed her to me, and we loaded up the car with our incredibly healthy, seemingly giant five-pound, twelve-ounce baby girl, homeward bound, free at last. Instantly, the past seemed to be a thousand years behind us. It was all a dream, and we were going home for the first time, just as if she had been born yesterday.

The next four days would be sheer bliss. We never put her down and sat in our new living room, babe in arms, looking out over the Pacific Ocean and feeling an indescribable state of joy. We had only a handful of visitors since the hospital had done a fantastic job of instilling the fear of germs into our entire beings.

On Friday evening, December 10, just four days later, we were watching the holiday movie Prancer on television. It ended as Santa crossed the sky and, simultaneously, Baby Isabella left our world peacefully in my arms dressed in her little snowflake outfit, with her daddy right beside me. The hours that followed were nothing less than sheer agony. Her daddy administered a heroic attempt at CPR as I screamed into the phone at the 911 operator.

The police were at the end of our street and were there in minutes. We passed our baby over to these experts pleading with them not to give up. The ambulance was there almost simultaneously, and shortly thereafter we found ourselves back at the hospital. The medical team was able to revive every organ in her body, every one that is except her brain.

As the horrible news spread, more and more family and friends gathered at the hospital. Several of Isabella's off-duty nurses arrived. Even my best friend from New York flew back to be with us. Then some twenty-four hours later, amidst all these loved ones, most of whom never got the chance to meet Isabella, together, we would set her spirit free to our singing voices. More than fifty people were in Isabella's hospital room, spilling out into the hallway, singing "You Are My Sunshine" through our tears, as the doctors unplugged her life-support system and gave her to me to hold in my arms one last time.

The days that followed were torturous. I felt as if it had somehow been my fault. We did not know what had happened. Had she suffocated in my arms? Had I missed a "desat"—the medical term that I had grown to know so well for what happens when a preemie "forgets" to breathe? But she had passed all of her tests? How on our watch did we lose her? Three days later we received a visit from the same amazing neonatologist who began our journey and the nurse who had implemented the massage study. They came to our home with the report from the medical examiner's office. It was SIDS, Sudden Infant Death Syndrome. This amazing man, in the same compassionate way, explained that even if she had been in the hospital in his hands, he could not have saved her.

Then he honored our daughter by telling us that he believed she was a Bodhisattva. In the Tibetan Buddhist tradition there is a title given: a Bodhisattva. This is reserved for an enlightened soul that delays Nirvana (entering heaven) and returns to Earth to help other souls. Sounds like an Angel to me.

I never had to bury a child. At first I thought that our experience at the hospital among family and friends was more like a memorial service and that would be enough. The thought of putting together a gathering of friends and family felt overwhelming, and then, it just happened. The Kanga Moms were on it. They transformed the church into a magical setting that gave tribute to a soul so great that there was no longer a need for her physical body. There were giraffes and pink balloons everywhere, including a four-foot-tall stuffed giraffe that we named IzB. My friends Karl and Jeanne Anthony, professional musicians, sang and my students read poems, sang and danced. Her godparents prayed us in and out. The minister, Rev. Wendy Craig-Purcell, was elegant and gave us strength by example. I put the outline together and Kanga Lori made the program titled "Isabella, Born to Dance with Angels."

I remembered how I felt when my best friend from high school had passed before her time. The priest asked me what we could do to make her funeral more special. At the time I thought it was an unusual question. Now I found myself asking Isabella the same question from my heart. Her heart spoke to mine and the answer was loud and clear: "Please Mommy, tell them all, thank you." I called my husband's mother and asked her to purchase white roses that we could hand out. One, two, better make it several dozen. We thanked our family and friends and my staff, and then asked if anyone was there from the hospital to please come forward. They just kept coming—more than two dozen nurses, doctors, and administrators were present for our little girl. We gave them each a rose and offered them a blessing. The room gave them a thunderous standing ovation. It was beautiful. I knew Isabella was pleased.

There was a slide show that introduced our daughter to our loved ones in attendance, five hundred or more. Most who attended never had the chance to meet her. The video technicians informed me that the slide show was tested and then re-tested again. It was perfect until the actual time it was to be played at the service. Two of the pictures were upside down. Those pictures had tremendous significance and personal meaning for me. I have heard it said that when spirits are present their vibrations interrupt our technology. (Since Isabella transitioned, I have had three computers completely crash and several other technically unexplained wonders that have made quite an impression on the most skeptical people I know.)

The only video we have of our daughter was taken by one of her amazing nurses for the hospital massage study. She was kind enough to put it to music, a beautiful rendition of "Somewhere Over the Rainbow" and "What a Wonderful World," performed by a Hawaiian singer named Israel "Iz" Kamakawiwo'ole. I had never heard it before except while watching her video. Just days after she left so peacefully in my arms, I went to a photography studio to get some of her pictures developed. I waited in the quiet lobby alone while the salesperson went to check the pictures on the disk. As soon as he left the room, the song came on. Someone in the back had started the CD player.

Tears immediately streamed down my face. I just knew there must be something in that lobby for me. As I turned around, I noticed a box of photographs for sale, photographs from Africa. I felt that there might be a giraffe picture in that box for me. I scrambled through the box and there it was. I purchased it and brought it home and showed it to my husband.

"Look what Isabella sent us today," I said.

He smiled and said, "Did you see your screen saver?"

I went to my computer and there was almost the identical picture without the giraffe. That morning he had taken the picture from our deck. Our little cabin that so mystically became ours is literally up in the treetops.

"Wow," I said, "the only thing that's missing is the giraffe."

"Not really," he said, "come take another look."

I stepped into our living room, gazing at the floor-to-ceiling windows that cover the back wall of our house. There on my living room floor, in the same place as the live giraffe in the picture, two-thirds of the way into the scene, is the four-foot-tall stuffed giraffe, IzB. It had been delivered by the Kanga Moms and placed right there after her memorial service; we had never moved it. What were the chances that the view from our living room would be treetops that would include a giraffe (okay, a stuffed giraffe) almost identical to this photograph from Africa? And that the Hawaiian singer Israel shared the same nickname, "Iz" that we called Isabella's giraffe and is also a popular nickname for Isabella?

The coincidences continued. Our new neighbors, Gerry and Melba, are penguin people. Gerry has made his career studying penguins in the Antarctic. He is also an exceptional and talented photographer. They had been unable to attend the memorial service and had come by for a visit. I gave them a copy of the program that had my thoughts about her spiritual umbilical cord when she was born. Melba said, "You know, I think I have something for you. I'll drop it in the mail." Then they were off to the South Pole.

Days later we received a card that had been professionally printed by a greeting card company. The cover was a photograph that Gerry had taken of nine fluffy baby penguins. There was one albino baby penguin in the center as white as snow. A crack in the glacier in the distance gave the illusion of a spiritual umbilical cord. On the back of the card the photo was titled, "Snowflake." I know that we are always connected. I don't need a cosmic two-by-four to hit me over the head; I have my Angels.

Is there a worse time of year to lose a loved one than the holiday season? I don't think so. Paralyzed by grief, we stayed home, taking turns sobbing our eyes out, wondering what happened—how did it all come crashing down so fast?

We dragged our swollen hearts to Drew's parents' home for the traditional holiday celebrations. I was resenting the responsibility and would have preferred to stay home, but we had three other daughters who needed a break from all the sadness.

I was having my well-deserved pity party, and now not only was I crushed over the passing of my baby, but who else could comfort my tears? I needed my mom. But my mom had made her transition years before Isabella was born.

My mother-in-law is a beautiful woman—kind and generous, with no hidden agenda, and no expectations. She is just pure love. She could have been a dancer—her legs go on forever. If I were to describe her in one word, it would be stunning. In two words, it would be amazingly thoughtful. At the beginning of the year we had gone shopping. She loves antiques and so I told her my misfortune of losing a valuable and sentimental Little Red Riding Hood cookie jar. It was the cookie keeper of my childhood, and because of my mother's illness it had disappeared with a number of other treasures years ago. I had always wanted to replace it, but even when you find one in an antique shop, the jar is priced well over $1,200, completely out of my budget.

Several months later she was shopping with a friend and found the collector's item. She purchased it and put it away. She was going to give it to me for my birthday, but something changed her mind, and she decided to save it for Christmas. There we were opening presents, and I could barely hold back the tears as I unwrapped this replica from my childhood. I could hardly believe my eyes. Knowing her frugality, I couldn't imagine her paying so much for a cookie jar. She smiled wryly and confessed, "The shopkeeper didn't know what he had."

For me the spirit of Christmas came alive that day, never to be silenced again. Somehow my mom so appropriately delivered a message through my other mother. If I could have heard her, I know she would be saying, "Don't worry, I'm here with Isabella and everything is going to be all right." How sweet it is to know that love knows no bounds.

# Chapter Three - Lessons from Isabella

*"She taught us to dedicate time to what's important ... And we found the joy of serving. She taught us to slow down ... and we found peace. She taught us to surrender ... and we found the unexpected surprises in letting go. She taught us to expose our hearts ... and we found true love."*

—*Lori Lorenz*

The holiday season blurred by and before I knew it, it was New Year's Eve and the sunset melted into amazing shades of orange and pink across the sky. My husband called to me, "Come look, Isabella has her paints out again." There had been an earlier tearful moment when the realization occurred to me that we would never be privy to all those wonderful pictures that children make for their parents. Now my husband pointed out that every day we get a hand-painted giraffe sunset!

I was planning on staying home with the baby for New Year's Eve while my husband and his first daughter went on a "date" to see her boyfriend and his band bring in the New Year. I decided that just because Isabella was in spirit didn't mean our plans should change. And besides, how often does an eighteen year old ask her dad out on a date? Staying home alone made my family and friends a little nervous. I assured them I would be fine and that I didn't feel alone. If I needed help, I knew that someone would be at my doorstep in minutes. All I would have to do is make the call.

The evening turned out to be one of the most creative nights of my life; born that night was my song to Isabella. Then for the first time I had the courage to go online and explore the available information on SIDS. I found "First Candle," a SIDS organization that supports the research of Dr. Hannah Kinney. Ten months later we had the privilege of meeting this incredible woman face to face at a conference in Washington DC. It turned out that Dr. Kinney has a theory that SIDS and a percentage of stillbirths might be related. Isabella passed the day before her actual due date. In Dr. Kinney's own words, she pondered the possibility that Isabella could have been a stillborn who lived! There is so much of life that can be revealed when we have the courage to live it all. There is so much that will remain a mystery regardless of what we do or think.

Shortly after the start of the new year, winter showed up in Southern California with mud slides and unusual torrential rains. We were driving home from a long weekend up north when we found ourselves stuck in traffic. The car traveled for only four miles in three hours! Most people would have gone out of their minds with frustration. My husband and I saw this as an opportunity to be together. We had a CD from Dr. Rev. Michael Beckwith that we had not had the chance to listen to. We popped it in the CD player. It was a beautiful, inspiring talk that left us feeling upbeat.

Toward the end of the CD, my husband started to daydream about how he could manage a private prayer session with this holy man. He thought that perhaps it would help me feel better. That's my husband—never thinking of himself. Just as he thought it, the voice of Dr. Reverend Michael played through the speakers; he said, "Let us pray for our loved ones … and for baby Isabella who left this earth too soon …" and he went on. Well, it turned out that he was not speaking about our Isabella, but hearing her name in prayer that way was all we needed. If we had not been "stuck" we might not have listened to the CD all the way to the end. We might not have been together when we heard it. It was a magical evening and the traffic made it perfect.

The torrential rains brought a flowering spring and spring is eternal! Kanga Lori decided to plant rosebushes in her backyard for Isabella and her niece, Maia Grace, who also had transitioned only ten hours after her birth the same year. A pink rosebush was planted for Maia and a white rosebush for Isabella. Isabella's plant needed extra TLC right from the start. In fact, it only had one full bloom, then lost its petals, never to bloom again. I had to buy Lori another rosebush since I felt responsible that "my kid" had messed with her garden.

When Nature speaks to me in this way, I try to listen. We are all unique manifestations of the one God. We have arrived on purpose with a purpose. That purpose is always the same, expressed in an infinite number of ways. We are here to release love into the atmosphere.

Labor Day, one year later, the Kanga families began a tradition to visit the hospital and bring a birthday party to Isabella's family of nurses and doctors. My husband and I were invited. We arrived at the front doors to find quite an entourage of children and adults garnished with homemade cookies and fudge.

The girls, under Kanga Katy's tutelage, had sewn giraffe pillows for the cuddlers (volunteers who hold the babies in the NICU) and families of the infants. Believe it or not, pillows in an intensive care unit to support your arms while you are holding a tiny baby are a precious commodity. Now every rocking chair would have its own Isabella Giraffe Pillow, made with extra love from some of the most talented dancers in San Diego.

However, the plan stopped there in the lobby. Now it was up to us to get permission to make this surprise delivery. They welcomed us with open arms. What a day of celebration and tears. It felt as though Isabella was with us as we walked the familiar halls on her birthday once again. Together, we birthed a new tradition. I love the vision of a pebble that is tossed into the lake; its ripples go on and on. Love knows no end. Isabella will never be forgotten.

We realized that having a SIDS attack while you are holding your baby is a very rare occurrence. Typically parents find their children in their crib. Perhaps we had something to offer other parents who were also suffering. We knew firsthand that this experience for the baby is painless. It happens in an instant. Isabella went to sleep and never woke up. She was silent, not even a squeak. Perhaps if we shared our experience, it could help ease the burden of guilt that so many parents come to know when faced with this tragedy. And perhaps by helping others, we would help ourselves to heal.

We created a presentation of our experience and ended it with "A Song for Isabella." I sang and her daddy played guitar. We first experimented with a dozen or so SIDS nurses in our area. They are a team of compassionate individuals who visit the home within days of this kind of nightmare. They suggested we go to Washington, DC for a conference. There, before a few hundred grieving parents, families, friends, and the medical community, we told our story and sang our song.

We knew we had made a difference. Afterward, people kept stopping us in the lobby wanting to know what kinds of things we were doing to feel better. They even asked for our CD. What CD? We are not professional songwriters; we're just grieving parents trying to heal. We were desperately trying to find the light in our dark world. Where was that precious little baby who was the light of life anyway? I just wanted to hold her and call out her name to see her smile one more time. My husband would say that he just wanted to smell her sweetness again. Perhaps she was right there with us, inspiring us to write more songs. It certainly seemed so.

We started to head home and arrived at the airport early, a remarkable experience for me since I am often challenged by time. We had two hours to fill. My husband and I sat looking out the windows as the planes took off when we got the idea. Let's make that CD they asked for. We immediately started to write another song right there in the airport. The words just poured onto my pad, and my husband put chords together and we began to sing. The joy was indescribable.

Suddenly, just then a small (perhaps a preemie?) commuter plane taxied by. On the side of the plane in big bold letters was the word SPIRIT. We were dazzled. Unsure if we had really seen this unusual sighting at just the right time, it returned in the other direction, SPIRIT. OK, so we didn't know that Southwest Airlines had a commuter airline on the East Coast named SPIRIT. Honestly, how do these magical coincidences occur? Obviously, as my mother would have said, "Only God knows!"

When we arrived home, we decided to have a party at our home and celebrate all of our friends who had birthdays in the fall, including Drew and Isabella. Kanga Katy made a cake, and I invited some of Isabella's baby friends from the NICU and their parents who we had met in the hospital. It was a magical evening. We sang songs and told stories all night long. Then the Kanga moms had a birthday gift to present to us for Isabella.

The Hurricane Katrina disaster had been heavy on our hearts. Kanga Lori was watching a news clip on television. There was a news report from a NICU in Louisiana, the camera angle unusual. The view was from behind what looked like the same four-foot stuffed giraffe in our living room that we had for Isabella's memorial service, our "IzB." The giraffe was looking at the babies. Lori describes it as if Isabella was talking to her and saying through the eyes of this giraffe, "Look at these babies, can you see them? You have to help them."

There were forty preemies that had been precariously evacuated to another hospital. The nurses hand-carried each of these tiny persons in canoes. Kanga Lori later found them in Baton Rouge. Together a selfless team created forty preemie packs, an orange canvas bag containing some necessary items: an outfit, diapers, a bookmark with "Lessons from Isabella," and most appropriately, a beautiful and cozy giraffe blanket, handmade by

Kanga Katy. They presented us with this prototype in honor of Isabella's birthday.

There was more love in that room that night than I could ever describe to you. In fact, there was overwhelming support from everyone in our lives. From the time we found out that we were having a baby until this moment has inspired us to rename SIDS. We no longer experience SIDS as Sudden Infant Death Syndrome, but Sudden Love.

It was time for cake and a picture. We keep Isabella's ashes in her room in a handmade wooden heart that her daddy made for her. I don't know why I said it, but I suggested to my husband, "Let's go get the baby." He mentioned that it might not be appropriate and perhaps even a little bit morbid. "Nonsense, it's the Kangas." We wrapped the heart containing Isabella's ashes in a blanket that one of the children had made for her so it would not be as conspicuous. We had never done anything like this before. So he took the heart and stood with the others behind the cake. He remembers vividly feeling all the love in the room and removed the blanket to expose the heart.

Kanga Carla, who had been Isabella's blood donor, snapped the picture. She looked at her view screen and gasped, "What's this?" Immediately, you could see it right there in the camera window. We all stood there amazed. We loaded it onto the computer and enlarged the area around Drew's face. With the exception of correcting Drew's red eye, the photo is untouched. You can see the most amazing phenomenon. We call the phenomenon "Isabella's Kiss"!

There are additional balls of light in the picture, not quite as magnificent as the one that rests on my husband's smile, but nevertheless they are there. We thought this was a one-of-a-kind event. How special that our little angel somehow showed up for her birthday party! Yet, in our hearts, we could not stop wondering what the deeper meaning could be.

One of our friends told us to research orbs. To our surprise there are thousands of people out there experiencing this photographic phenomenon. We went back and looked through our pictures since her passing. There they were—brilliant balls of light. We just never noticed them before. Since then we have taken hundreds of pictures and have been blessed by hundreds of sightings. Today, we truly feel that we all are surrounded by angels!

November 1 was right around the corner. This was the one-year anniversary when we played dress-up for Halloween at the hospital with Isabella. Kanga Lori had taken more pictures of our girl than any paparazzi in Hollywood. We didn't know that the pictures we would take on this day would become Isabella's "angel picture" that you find on the cover of this book! It was not an easy day for me. I had to call for help. I called the Kanga Moms and told them that I didn't think I was going to make it through the day.

They appeared, appropriately dressed in giraffe orange. They had brought a "grief picnic" in their car and off we went to find a grassy spot. It turned out to be a parking lot under a street light. There they pulled out of their basket a blanket, treats, and an art project. We placed Isabella's little Halloween costume in a shadow box that I could display in her room forever. The costume was an American Girl Doll, Swan Lake Costume, the angel halo from Target. We told Isabella stories, and laughed and cried until we wore ourselves out. Grief can turn your emotions into waves like an ocean. The giant ones do not last forever and any attempt to surf them can take you for a tumble. It is important to ask for help when you need it.

Suddenly it was December. It was time for another Nutcracker, except this year when the show was over we could not go pick up our sweet Isabella from the hospital. There are no words to describe the deep sorrow that the culmination of this first year revealed. When the anniversary of her transition had passed, I knew it was time to move forward, together, in a new way. It was now a new year.

Our tiny baby daughter, Isabella, born breathing on her own at one pound, eleven ounces, taught me three things of which I am sure. The first: God is all there is. The second: Teilhard de Chardin was brilliant when he said, "We are spiritual beings having a human experience." The third: grief is a gift. Grief is one of the most powerful emotions that we have for learning and deepening our understanding for ourselves, each other, and our world. Once the gift has been delivered, it is never returned, and our fundamental way of learning is catapulted into PhD-level work.

My past losses have taught me that you cannot ignore grief. You cannot medicate It, stuff It, or pretend It never happened. What we can do is become awake to It. Embrace It. Live with It. Laugh with It and cry with It. In time, It will transform and reveal our true selves in ways we could not have imagined before It. Grief is the missing key that unlocks the evolution of human spirit. Lucky me, I was given the key over and over again. I resisted for many years and then, thanks to Isabella, I finally let go of my fears, walked through the door and, as inspirational speaker and best-selling author Dr. Wayne Dyer has said, "I was no longer nowhere, but nowhere."

Isabella has inspired me to tell my stories of death and dying and what has helped me move through my darkest nights of the soul. I prefer to call death "transition," for science tells us that energy is neither created nor destroyed, it merely changes form. Our religious philosophies have always boasted about life everlasting. For me, our souls, energies of love, a love that never dies, continue on and behold the capacity to still communicate. Perhaps the easiest way for us to listen is to notice a coincidence. We all have them. It is my desire that these stories inspire you to "stay awake" and notice the coincidences in your life journey that point out the opportunities where we all learn to grow and stretch.

One more thing Isabella taught me is that life is not comfortable—life is an adventure. Today, I approach life the way her daddy enters the kitchen. He transforms whatever is available into a gourmet meal. He mixes pounds of passion, gallons of joy, together with overflowing cupfuls of patience. He stirs in understanding, sprinkles with tears, and tops with love!

Bon appétit!

# Chapter Four - My Grandmother, Angela

*"The warmth of an angel's light can comfort and illuminate the whole world."*

—*Anonymous*

Today in the twenty-first century, if someone told you they had been visited by an angel, your response might be sarcastic: "Have you been watching that TV show again?" And, if that visit had brought a miraculous healing, there might be a sense of disbelief, and then hope, cancelled out by thoughts of the ridiculous, the absurd, or a coincidence—or you might think that person is just plain crazy. Perhaps we need to rethink our cynicism and be open to the possibility that we all may be surrounded by Angels.

I was named Angela after my mother's mother. Sadly, my mother found out she was pregnant shortly after my grandmother had passed away. I met my grandmother through the stories my mother told me. She painted a picture of an independent, courageous woman who came to America through Ellis Island when she was only nineteen years old. Her travel companions were her husband and their six-month-old daughter, Angelina. Thanks to the Internet, I proudly keep the ship's manifest framed in my office. Once in America, the couple had four more children. Then, in the midst of the Great Depression, my grandfather died of pneumonia. Angela, with no education, raised five children alone by sewing at home for the factories.

I grew up disappointed that I did not get to play with this woman. Yet, thanks to those stories, my grandmother always felt very alive to me. One summer, when I was around fourteen years old, my mother was stricken with a crippling arthritis attack. She had been in bed for almost two weeks, unable to walk.

I loved to sing and play the piano. After a long, hot day of helping take care of my mom, I would go into the living room and play the piano until it was very late. My mother had decorated the living room with a typical New York Italian flare. A 10-foot long, red velvet couch with plastic covers monopolized the far wall. Hanging in the corner was a lamp with red stained glass that gave the room a warm glow, especially in August.

There was this one particular evening when I was singing and playing when suddenly the room got very cold. It sent a shiver down my spine. I stopped playing and looked behind me. The room was washed in the glow from the lamp, and it really felt like my grandmother's spirit was hovering around that lamp. No, I didn't really see anything. However, I did acknowledge her presence in my mind.

I asked, "Grandma, have you come to make my mom feel better and hear me sing?"

I did not get an answer, so I just started to play again. By the end of the song the room was no longer cold.

The next morning was another hot, East Coast summer morning. As the sun rose and shined through the sheer white curtains, the air hung thick and you knew it was going to be a scorcher. It was impossible to sleep in, so there I was, first thing in the morning, back at the piano again. Suddenly, my mother came running in. She shouted, "Angela, Angela, it's a miracle, it's a miracle, I'm all better." She was jumping up and down. I smiled and gave her a big hug, yet inside my teenage mind I was completely freaked out. It took me weeks to tell her my version of what had happened the night before. I will never forget the expression on her face that so much wanted to believe that it could be true.

What was it that healed my mother that day? Was it my grandmother? Was it a miracle? Was it God? Was it a coincidence? For me it was all of it. The common denominator of these possibilities was love. For me, the energy of love, brought forth by whatever you might call the intelligence that turns an acorn into an oak tree everytime was ever present. I felt it. It transformed a young girl's thoughts and placed her on the road less traveled.

# Chapter Five -
# Elaine, My Best Friend

*"Sometimes your best friend is actually a guardian angel in disguise."*
—*Anonymous*

Elaine was my best friend in high school. Our personalities complemented each other and we had something very special in common, uncommon for teenagers in the seventies. We were drug-free and devoted Italian Catholics. Elaine introduced me to what was then called "The Christian Awakening Program." The program was run by the Diocese of Rockville Center. It was a four-day weekend retreat for teenagers, developed by a psychologist that explored the relationship between a young person and God. I was inspired by how I would apply what I discovered about myself to my world. It was a life-changing experience for me. We were both invited back to be leaders and give talks during future weekends.

Elaine wanted to be a nurse—an unrealized dream for a beautiful person who was born with a heart defect. She would have been the perfect candidate for a heart transplant, but in 1960 the technology had not yet arrived. It was hard for her to breathe, and she often took breaks when she slowly walked the halls of our high school.

What her body lacked in strength, her spirit overcompensated. Wherever Elaine went, she made a difference. She never complained and never let on that she did not share the same life expectancy as her peers. Elaine was vital and alive with a love for life that took my breath away. I loved hanging out with her. Her joy was contagious, her friendship a blessing. I wanted to be a Broadway dancer—a "gypsy" was the professional term. I studied dance for four to six hours a day at the professional dance studios in Manhattan. Elaine went away to college in Connecticut, about an hour drive from our hometown on Long Island. Her parents, two of the most amazing people I have ever met, let her live her life on her terms. She treasured her relationship with them.

On the weekends I would often drive up to see her. Elaine loved a party. College life on Friday and Saturday nights provided the fun and excitement that Elaine had missed growing up inside an unwilling physical form. However, college life was taking its toll on her frail, yet spirited body. It was difficult for her to walk to her classes and keep up with the other students.

It was the spring of her second year, my birthday weekend, and I decided to stay home.

I thought it was odd that she had not called me. There were no cell phones in those days and, although I tried, I could not reach her or her family. Returning from a day at the beach, I came home to find my mother crying uncontrollably. I knew it must be Elaine. I remember asking if she was at the hospital; I would go immediately and at least hold her hand and say good-bye. My mother shook her head. It was too late. She was already gone.

This was my first experience with sudden death. I could remember wailing and screaming all over the house, together with my mom. I was crushed to my core. Inconsolable, I spoke to my beloved best friend in my mind and asked her this question: "Elaine, if the afterlife was as wonderful as they have taught us, could you please send me a sign? I don't need fire and brimstone, just a small sign."

I attended her wake in a state of disbelief—myself and hundreds of others. Elaine had touched the hearts and souls of so many. How could this be happening? I thought I was watching a movie, I felt so detached. The funeral was early the next morning and Elaine's parents asked me to ride with the family. Before I left the funeral parlor, the priest asked me if I could think of anything that would make Elaine's funeral more special. "Special?" I quipped. "Funerals are not special!" I was so angry and thought he was out of his mind. I told him no and went home in the rain, completely brokenhearted, I really don't know how I got home safely. Something bigger than me guided my car as the rain pounded and my tears poured.

A couple of months earlier Elaine had been home for the weekend. She had gone to church without me and called me as soon as it was over. She was so excited and told me about this amazing singer who played the guitar and sang the song "Be Not Afraid." It turned out that the singer's name was Kathy and her voice was exceptional. I had never met Kathy or heard the song, yet suddenly on that treacherous drive home from the funeral parlor, the song sang sweetly in my mind. Could that be the "something special" that the priest had been looking for? I cried harder.

When I arrived home I felt anxious, and even though it was very late I called the rectory. I told the priest that Elaine had been at church a few months ago and was so impressed with this one particular singer who sang the song "Be Not Afraid." I didn't know her name but perhaps he would remember? Wouldn't that be wonderful if she could sing for Elaine? He thanked me and we hung up.

I don't remember how I slept, if at all. Consumed with grief when I arrived at Elaine's house the next morning, I had forgotten all about the events of the night before. I rode with the family to the church. It was pouring again. I thought, "Even the angels are devastated." We arrived at the church. There was nothing to prepare me for what came next.

There must have been a thousand or more in attendance. From elementary school friends to college acquaintances, we gathered from near and far. I walked down the aisle behind the casket draped in white, my eyes blurred by tears. It oddly felt more like her wedding than her funeral. Then, as I looked up at the altar; I saw eight priests standing there to con-celebrate her service. She was royalty, she had been so much to so many, and she was my best friend.

I left her casket before the altar and took my seat feeling completely numb. As I gazed upon the scene and saw all of these holy men in regal white robes, I was overtaken by such beauty. These are the ones we turn to for comfort and wisdom. Here they stood in all the fanfare that a church could muster. I searched their faces to find answers for why these things have to happen. Their solemn expressions made me feel that they too were at a loss for how they would bring honor to this young woman and peace to the crowd. It felt so surreal, so sad, and so beautiful all at the same time.

I felt my chest tighten and realized that I was barely breathing. Again the magnificence and the grandeur of so many people gathered in our grief, still celebrating who she was, seemed bigger than life to me. I inhaled this beauty like it was pure oxygen. Then I took another look, and I noticed in the far corner a woman standing there, oh so quietly with her guitar. I was shocked. Somehow between 11 pm the night before and early this morning, the priest had managed to reach her and, even more miraculously, she was available.

My heart raced. It was my small yet so significant sign. The funeral continued and when it was time for communion, the priest motioned for the guitarist to begin. She started to walk to her place but the organist played a resounding chord from up in the balcony and the planned singer upstairs began her rendition of Ave Maria. The priest relieved the panic of this selfless volunteer in front of him and nodded for her to wait. And then after the lines of broken hearts filed through and communion was over, the guitarist walked center stage and sang to all of us like an angel. It was a concert, orchestrated from a world beyond, and there was not a dry eye in the house.

Elaine was an Earth Angel, and her funeral was a glorious celebration of a life well-lived. There was more life and love packed into her short nineteen years than most people ever experience.

On the way to the cemetery, Elaine's parents said that it felt as if Elaine were singing it herself, right to them. How right they were. My journey in faith continued.

# Chapter Six -
## My Only Sister, Nancy Jeanne

*"Make yourself familiar with the angels and behold them frequently in spirit; for without being seen, they are present with you."*
—St. Francis de Sales

I was the thing in the yellow basket. For my sister, twelve and a half years my senior, the permanent visit of such a creature was justly called. There are not many fond memories of growing up with my sister. I can recall one incident when I was perhaps three or four years old. She and her friends acted as if I had disappeared. I remember stomping my feet and shouting, "I am here, I am here," their laughter tormenting me. By the time I was five, she was off to college, then marriage. She managed to keep her distance from the family. My parents adored her unconditionally, and I always hoped that someday, just maybe, she would like me.

The day came. It was my high school graduation and I received a card in the mail. It was the typical Nancy, a humorous, non-intimate kind of card. Yet, this time it was different. Snoopy, by Charles M. Schultz, was on the cover and inside, written by her hand, was a small note. "Angela, if you ever need a wall to bounce your thoughts off of, let me know." I was inspired. Perhaps now in my soon-to-be-adult life we could find the sisterhood I had longed for.

Three months later, my sister—a giant athlete and talented musician who was twelve credits away from achieving a PhD in music education—awoke one morning unable to walk, completely paralyzed on her right side. They called it an inoperable, malignant brain tumor, an astrocytoma. Devastation swept through the family. Even today the prognosis for such a tumor is a death sentence, with a life expectancy averaging three to four months. My sister, with the help of an overdose of radiation, fought back and suffered indescribably for thirteen years. What could be the meaning for this kind of agonizing existence? The cancer destroyed my sister's body but not her soul. Later, I would be blessed to feel the love that set her spirit free.

Nancy had married a man who also did not possess a personality that I would describe as warm and fuzzy. To their credit, Italian families from New York can be a little overwhelming, even suffocating, especially to young newlyweds. My sister and her husband had escaped to Chicago. This challenged the support system for a family now faced with the unimaginable charge of helping her move through the pain of a terminal illness.

We were not graceful in our efforts. My mother developed Alzheimer's and ultimately was unable to make the trip from New York to Chicago to help in her care. My father suffered multiple heart attacks and was paralyzed by grief. Helpless, he could not bear to see his daughter exist in such pain. And me, I had gotten married and divorced for all the wrong reasons and was now a single mother, raising my daughter alone in Southern California.

It was a warm summer day in August, and I was sitting on the beach with a musician buddy who was visiting from New York. We looked out over the Pacific Ocean, and I felt a sense of serenity that was remarkably unfamiliar. I began to sing to my friend the song my sister wrote, "What Is Love." After an extraordinary sunset, we returned to my home. The message was waiting. My sister had transitioned at the precise time that I sang her song out to the deep blue ocean. The days that followed were equally awe-inspiring.

My sister's funeral had taken place in Chicago without the Italian brigade. My daughter and I flew back to New York where the family gathered for a small, informal memorial service. My parents, my daughter, and I sat quietly in the front row of the church, my mother's siblings behind us. Now, as I sat in this surreal experience, I felt something was missing. My little Italian momma, aka the Alzheimer's patient, was completely calm. No wailing, no tears, a seemingly inner peace. My mind raced; I thought, "It must be drugs."

Evaluating the situation, I turned around and demanded that my aunts tell me what they had given her, valium perhaps, and how much? Whatever it was, it was working, and I was actually afraid of an accidental overdose. It would be just our luck to have an emergency room visit right then. If Aunt Betty just gave her a little, and then Aunt Jenny gave her a little, and then Uncle Jack … well, you get the picture. I searched their faces for hints of guilt. A resounding and innocent denial of any such thing was returned to me. We were in church, so I believed them.

I could not help but ask my mother gently, "Mom, you're so calm, how are you doing it?"

She replied, "I'm really OK. I feel like Nancy's spirit is hovering over those candles."

As I looked back on the altar to view the candles, I could not believe my eyes. Twinkling silver lights were hovering over the flames. It was breathtaking. In disbelief, I whispered into my seven-year-old daughter's ear, "Jeanne Marie, do you notice anything unusual about the altar?"

She replied with a child's innocent whisper, "You mean those silver lights over the candles?"

That was enough for me. My mother felt it. We saw it. All at once I knew, "There are more things in heaven and earth, Horatio, than are dreamt of in your philosophy." Shakespeare knew it too, and I think he was right.

# Chapter Seven -
# Dragonfly, Send Me Your Love

*"To love for the sake of being loved is human, but to love for the sake of loving is angelic."*

—*Alphonse Marie de Lamartine*

I loved my daddy. I don't know when, if ever, he recovered from his disappointment that I wasn't a boy. But I do know that he never purposefully let on to me. I figured all that out later with my support team. While my dad walked this earth, I never needed my ego. I had my daddy's eyes that gleamed with pride. Regardless of what I did, he always seemed so proud. He would walk around in life telling everyone that he was "Angela's Father." Yet, for me, he was so much more. He was my confidant, my support, my personal comedian, my silent business partner, my teacher, and my best friend. He was Pop-Pop to my first daughter when her own father was emotionally unavailable. He was my hero.

By the time I was thirty-five, my mother's mental condition and his heart were deteriorating quickly. I began to feel an inner panic. I was just not ready for him to die. I went to a spiritual advisor, expecting her to have a crystal ball that would tell me that this relentless suffering would soon heal itself, and we could all live happily ever after. Instead, her tone changed, and she said, "It takes nine months for us to prepare for the birth of a baby and yet rarely does anyone help us prepare to transition back." In that brief instant my job description changed; my angst vanished. I no longer felt the anxiety and burdened responsibility of finding the right doctor, the right medication, and the secret to keeping this giant alive in his body—a body that clearly had all the signs that it was almost all used up.

I began to ask the question, "What would it look like to prepare someone for a journey back to spirit? And the answers came. My father was afraid of dying. I took him to church one Sunday, and the minister told a story about water bugs. From that day on, our conversations were real, playful, philosophical, mystical, and filled with deep sharing from the heart. The minister's story of transformation became the foreshadowing of what was yet to come.

## The Water Bugs

*A colony of water bugs lived in the muck and mire at the bottom of a lily pond. They were happy, normal, everyday water bugs. Happy that is, except for one mystery.*

*They could not understand why every now and then one of them would crawl up the stem of the lily pad and never be seen again.*

*So, one day, one of the members of the water bug colony called a meeting of the whole group.*

*He said, "Look, this keeps happening. And we still don't understand it. Let's make a pact right now that the next one of us that crawls up one of the stems of these lilies will come back and tell the rest of us what has happened to him."*

*Well, a few weeks later, the water bug who called the meeting felt an irresistible urge to climb the stem of the lily pad **toward the light he could barely see**. And he began to do just that. Laboriously, he made the journey and in time he found himself on top of the lily pad. He was exhausted. But, as he lay there, he experienced the warmth and brightness of the sunlight—a whole new experience for him—and he fell asleep.*

*When he awoke, he found himself encased in a stiff, brittle coating, but something in him urged him to beat against it with all his might. The hard shell began to crack, and soon he emerged a **beautiful blue green dragonfly**. He began skimming over the surface of the pond on his new gleaming wings. As he flew back and forth across the pond looking down into it, he could imagine his friends and family there still in the muck, still water bugs. Happy enough ... but wondering whatever happened to him.*

*He realized, "I can't go back, I can't. I can't tell them. But, one day each of them will discover for themselves what has happened to me, and they will have the same experience."*

*     *     *

That story seemed to lift our spirits to a new level of awareness, a new vibration for communication. My father also enjoyed a good mystery. I had him read *The Celestine Prophecy* by James Redfield. The book is an adventure story, a modern-day parable. It has many levels of understanding. My father really enjoyed it, and our respect for each other and God grew bigger, with more meaningful appreciation for life than I had ever felt before.

There is a section in the book that describes how everyone can train their eyes to see auras. An aura is the energy field that surrounds all living things. It can be seen in many different colors. My dad must have taken this section seriously and began to practice. One day I was picking him and my mom up from a doctor's visit. As usual, I was in a hurry. I found them sitting outside of the building on a park bench like two teenagers. My dad was lying down with his head in my mom's lap, staring at the grass and playing with his sunglasses. "Green glass, clear glass, what color is the grass?" he thought. I watched from a distance wondering what in the world he was doing. I was quickly losing my patience. He was ignoring me and continuing with his little game, not realizing that I was going to be late for work.

He finally got up and walked slowly with my little Alzheimer's mom in tow. He got to the car and peered through the open window. The expression on his face had an unfamiliar feeling of a new kind of wisdom. He reminded me of the scene in the movie The Ten Commandments and how different Charlton Heston looked after seeing the burning bush. His tone was serious. "Ang," my father said, "the grass is gold." We drove home in silence.

The days that followed were hectic. I was building a new dance studio, and I was really busy with all that goes into the construction and growing pains of a small business. It was just three days after Father's Day. Because of my heavy work schedule, I had not spent the quality time with my dad that I had longed for. I was envisioning that when I finished teaching that night, I would drive to the video store, pick up a Western, and spend the evening watching television and holding his hand.

At exactly ten minutes to 8 pm, I was choreographing the finale to the environmental children's show I had written called "Earthkalah." I had my students center floor, trying to work out a circular pattern, when I looked up and through the large, roll-up garage door I saw out in the alley an old man in a white T-shirt wearing blue jeans. His face seemed fuzzy and unrecognizable in the twilight. It felt creepy that we were being watched in our leotards by this stranger. I knew that I must go out there and tell him, in my New York attitude, to get lost. As I stepped onto the asphalt, he disappeared right before my eyes. I let out a scream and the girls who had been lost in their dancing came running to my rescue. We looked up and down that alleyway. There was no one there. Seconds later the phone rang—it was my neighbor with instructions to come right home.

The scene that met my eyes when I reached home was from a movie. The ambulance, the fire department, my dear friend Deb, and a handful of neighbors were all there. Deb, a real live angel, had called my parents to offer a meal since I was working late. When my mom asked my dad (who was sitting by himself watching television) what he wanted for dinner, and he didn't respond, she panicked. Then in her Alzheimer's state she dropped the phone and ran out of the house screaming to get a neighbor. Deb, on the end of the phone, heard her despair and came right over.

By the time I got there, the paramedics were talking to him, and he was still not responding. We all jumped into the ambulance and took that ride to the hospital. My dad's wishes were always to do everything medically possible; however, hours later technology revealed that he had had a massive brain hemorrhage and would not recover. We let him go to our singing voices, one song after another, including his favorite, "You Are My Sunshine."

So there I was, in a hospital room with my hero at peace, my teenage daughter at my side, and my mother in a terminal state of forgetfulness. It was a transformational moment in time. One moment I felt like a small child completely abandoned, the next an adult, solely responsible for the well-being of the women who loved him so deeply. I was so scared.

When morning came, the nightmare that I hoped was a dream turned out to be real. My dad was still gone, and I had to make all those preparations that we as humans do when someone passes. I now had no siblings and the nearest family member was three thousand miles away.

Shopping for caskets—now there is an experience that no one ever prepares you for. I was a woman, aka professional shopper. I had been shopping for most of my life, but never had anyone mention to me that there was a casket store. I was first in shock that there even was such a place. Yet there in the belly of the funeral parlor was a furniture showroom, with about fifty or more samples in a variety of styles and colors, and let's not forget the interiors. How long was I supposed to peruse, let alone make a decision? I cried inconsolably, to no surprise of the salesperson, who was fully prepared with a box of tissues. I finally settled on an elegant, yet modest, mahogany variety whose manufacturer's tag claimed they planted a tree in your loved one's honor. Supporting the environment somehow brought me peace in my awkward decision process.

I had the additional responsibility of having to bring my dad back to the East Coast in his "new home" for the traditional wake and funeral. On the flight back, sitting in my seat, I felt numb. My thoughts faded back—back forty-eight hours. Back to the dance studio, back to choreographing the finale for "Earthkalah." Back to the children dancing and then I saw him, the man standing in the alley. Who was he? What was he? Now in my stillness I traced my memory, the blue jeans, the white T-shirt—that was my father's favorite outfit! That's what he wore on his last ride in the ambulance to the hospital. His facial features lost in the twilight, then the image disappearing in a flash. Had my dad come to say good-bye? I had heard of stories like this before. I drifted off to sleep in wonder.

Arriving in New York, I no longer felt alone. My father's presence was everywhere. We arrived late at my parents' home on Long Island. My aunt had already been there to leave a fresh pot of meatballs and gravy (real Italians call red sauce gravy) on the stove to welcome us home. The details of the days that followed seemed to be divinely guided and went as smoothly as could be expected—even surprisingly well, without the anticipated drama. We placed my hero to rest, and now it was my turn to have a few days alone.

A dear family friend suggested I visit an ashram in upstate New York. My aunts would take care of my mom, and my daughter would visit her father. There was no reason not to go. My friend and I drove for a few hours and stopped for breakfast at the Red Apple, the same restaurant that had become a breakfast tradition on the way to visit my sister in college. I hadn't been there since I was a little girl. Suddenly life felt familiar and light.

I had never been to an ashram before. I felt humbled and blessed to be visiting such holy ground at this sensitive time in my life. It was truly a beautiful place. I watched in awe as Guru

Mai blessed the devotees with peacock feathers. Simultaneously, without a sound, the children played at her feet, while the adults sang beautiful holy chants. When we left this temple of peace, it was time for dinner.

Marvelous vegetarian cuisine was waiting in the nearby restaurant. As my friend and I studied the menu out front, a small man with a fabulous Irish accent approached us and said, "Excuse me, but I really think you should try the restaurant on the other side of the campus. You will enjoy the walk." Then he was gone as quickly as he came. My friend and I looked at each other and giggled as if we had just been visited by a leprechaun and decided to go for the walk.

Before long we were on a trail that brought us into a lush East Coast forest. The canopy was so green. Suddenly, I heard the sound of running water. I began to run, expecting to find a bubbling brook. I found the brook and a small walking bridge that crossed it. The bridge was brand new, made completely of raw wood. There was no finish on it at all. It felt as though a carpenter had just completed it in time for us to cross it and might be watching us from behind a tree to see if we liked it. I ran to the center of the bridge and to my surprise, I looked down and there were hundreds of beautiful delicate blue-green dragonflies hovering frantically over the water. Just like in the story, the water bug, now turned blue-green dragonfly, wanted so much to go back and tell his friends and family what had happened to him. The story jumped off the page and came to life for me, and so did my dad.

From that day forward, dragonflies miraculously began to appear at the most amazing times in my life. They show up in a variety of styles. Sometimes they come from the paintings of my students or maybe someone is wearing a pair of dragonfly earrings. One time a colleague even gave me the gift of a dragonfly kitchen sink drain cover. Then there are the times they just fly by. Hundreds and hundreds of sightings have arrived at the most extraordinary times in my life. Even now, so many years later, they continue to magically arrive. This sweet connection that I have with my dad is truly indescribable.

They say that a coincidence is when two or more things coincide at precisely the right time. No, my dad's not a bug. But I do believe we all have angels, and mine just love to send me signs so I can remember that I am never alone.

# Chapter Eight - Flutter by, Butterfly

*"And flights of angels sing thee to thy rest."*
*—William Shakespeare, Hamlet*

I've mentioned that my parents were Italian, and being part of a big Italian family, I could not escape the concept of transition. Back then we called it death and dying; now I know better. There was always somebody coming or going, and I've had to attend big Italian funerals since I was a little girl. In fact, a giant memory in my childhood is that my parents were always talking about, "When I die …" and what their wishes might be. I think those childhood experiences were the foreshadowing of my life story.

My mother showed signs of Alzheimer's by the time I was seventeen years old. She was formally diagnosed when I was twenty-six. Living with and being the caregiver for an Alzheimer's patient is unusual to say the least. My father found it difficult to care for her alone, and so my parents would come to "visit" my daughter and me in San Diego—short visits that only lasted about six to nine months at a time! I hope you can feel my desire to keep my sense of humor during these incredibly long and challenging times.

We always had to have our eyes wide open to make sure my mom was safe. She loved to clean. One evening, as my daughter and I drove up to our house, we found more than a dozen large green garbage bags outside by the curb. They were not filled with trash but with our personal items: the contents of my closet, clothes, shoes ... all of my daughter's toys. The house was clean.

I find that when I am willing to "stay awake," the beauty of life always reveals a rainbow after a storm. I finally had to place my mother in a nursing home six months after my father's passing. My mother never wanted to be placed in a nursing home. Knowing that it was not her wishes made this one of the most difficult things I ever had to do. I had my mother on a waiting list for years for what I had decided, after careful consideration, was the best nursing care facility in town.

It was early in January when my mom had one of her most challenging days. Clearly, as a single mom, I could not provide a safe haven for this Alzheimer's patient. The very next day, the call came: a room was available at the nursing home. Delivering my mother to a place she never envisioned herself, while she was still healthy, was agonizing. Intellectually, I knew it was the right thing to do. As a daughter, however, I felt like a failure.

There I was alone in the office with the director of administration, filling out more paperwork and trying to read the fine print through my tears; then I just about fell off my chair. The unit that my mother would be staying in was called "Penn Station." Last time I checked, Penn Station was three thousand miles away in New York, where my mother commuted daily as a young girl. What were the chances that after years of trying to avoid this day, we would arrive back at "Penn Station"? It was as if something bigger than me told me it was going to be OK. I cried with relief. A few weeks later they remodeled and renamed the wing "Wellington Hall." Mmmmm ... timing is everything!

Four years later, just days before my fortieth birthday, my dear friend and personal assistant, Miss Donna, took me to lunch. There she presented me with a gift. It was not meant to be a birthday present. However, there it was in all its glory: "The Dragonfly Story" as a child's picture book, a version with the most beautiful illustrations. She had purchased it in Hawaii several months before and we just had not made the time for this exchange. So there he was, my hero, sending his love again. This time the message was bigger, but I didn't realize that until later.

The very next day, Donna and I spent the morning and early afternoon working outside in a friend's backyard. It was an unusual spring day as there were butterflies, seemingly hundreds of butterflies, all over that yard. They were just hanging there, all over the patio cover. To be honest, it felt a little creepy, like the plague of the butterflies from a soon-to-be-released Alfred Hitchcock movie. It felt like something was about to happen, but I couldn't imagine what it could be.

Later that afternoon, I got the call from the nursing home that I had been dreading for as long as I could remember. My Mom had lapsed into a coma, and I needed to go to the nursing home as soon as possible. I raced home and gathered all my necessary items that I would need while sitting with my mother until her very last breath: my favorite Bible, prayer books, and music. I felt so prepared; after all, by now I was beginning to feel like an expert in transition.

At the time, I was living on the coast, and so I had to travel a quaint country road east, until I reached the nursing home that was inland. As I drove, butterflies enveloped my car. It was difficult to drive. Through my tears I could see their wings fluttering everywhere. My cell phone rang, and it was Donna. She too had raced home and turned on the news. It seems that once every ten years the Painted Lady Butterfly migrates from Mexico to Oregon. Up until then, I had always wondered why my mother lingered for so many years with this disabling disease. Now it seemed as if she had been waiting for just the right moment so I could understand. That day it became clear, a cosmic giggle from my mom.

Now you might think that it was just a coincidence. Knowing my parents, I think that they were just a little bit more on purpose. They were proud and loved to throw a little competition into their marriage. I started to fantasize and could just imagine them bantering. My Dad would say, "Jeanne, when I die, I am going to send Angela a dragonfly at just the right time so that she knows how much I love her." My mom quips back and says, "Oh yeah, Jimmy, well, I'm not going to die until thousands of butterflies are available to show Angela just how much I love her." And that is exactly what she did.

The story doesn't end there. Two weeks later, I was going through an unusual divorce. That is a story for another book. For now, try to imagine that I was sitting in an attorney's office who was evaluating my situation. She pointed out rather frankly that all of my finances were no longer in my name; every penny that I had ever worked for and invested, and all of my father's inheritance, was gone. My soon to be ex-husband of less than two years was a financial advisor who we now could determine had alternative reasons for marrying me, none that seemed to include love. She let me know very clearly that I was in big trouble. I guess I needed to have known about, studied, and listened to Suze Orman before I started my life as an adult.

Still grieving over my father and then my mom after she entered the nursing home, I managed to marry a man I barely knew. Vulnerable and naïve is a great explanation, but still leaves me responsible for saying yes to a proposal that created my financial demise. In less than two years this man managed to embezzle my father's inheritance and every penny I had ever worked for. I was financially devastated. Equally devastating is that the attorney, realizing I needed immediate assistance, could not help me since she was leaving town. I would have to find someone else.

I drove home in a state of shock and landed on the wrong freeway going in the wrong direction. In retrospect, I was in no shape to be driving. I was minutes away from my church, and so I continued to that destination. When I arrived, I was in awe of the hundreds of people in a line circling the building. Apparently, a popular speaker named James Van Praagh was presenting for the evening. I had never heard of him before and began to hear an excited chatter growing amongst the crowd. Apparently this gentleman talks to dead people. I was not impressed. However, since I believe that there really are no accidents, and since I had no intention of ever being there, I decided to stay. Actually I was feeling sorry for myself, and I realized that in my emotional state I should not be driving.

The ticket was $75. I had my last $100 bill in my wallet, all the money I had left in the world. It was too late to turn back. I paid for my ticket and the usher, a friend of mine, secured me a place in the front row. We were seated an hour before the start time. It takes a while to seat a thousand people. I had no idea what to expect. I did appreciate the opportunity to just sit, wait, and try and clear my head of the recent drama.

Then they announced Mr. Van Praagh. He spoke for two hours on spirituality 101. It was nice, but I looked around and thought … a thousand people, $75 a person, hey, maybe I should try this. After a fifteen-minute break, I was about to be humbled. I took notes; this is pretty much what he said verbatim.

James, using his hands to make graceful gestures, said, "Spirits vibrate at a frequency that is much faster than humans. Since I was a young child, I seemed to have been given this gift of having guides to translate for me. So if something sounds familiar, raise your hand and we'll give you a microphone and we'll talk. Like for instance, if your name is Angela." My blood ran cold. I looked around the room: one thousand people and he didn't say Mary or Susie, a more common example. He said "Angela," and it was in a tone that remarkably resembled my mom when she was trying to get my attention. He started to give some other directions when he was clearly interrupted by a voice in his head. Waving his arms he said impatiently, "All right, all right. So, for instance, if your mother just died and your name is Angela." I jumped to my feet, tears streaming down my face, waving my hand like a kindergartner, "My mother just died April 24, and my name is Angela."

The room's occupants delivered a resounding hush in awe. James remained calm and a bit condescending. He said with attitude, "Oh, you're the one. I know all about it. Your mother came to me in a meditation when I was up in the chapel" (the very chapel where I had had my mother's memorial service days earlier). He continued, "Just sit down and relax, you're as pushy as your mom. Don't worry, I will get to you." All righty then, I sat down and waited patiently, somewhat embarrassed and in a state bewilderment.

The best I can tell you is that for the next forty-five minutes, James Van Praagh channeled my mother and several other relatives from the other side, delivering extremely personal messages by name and by event, recent events that I had not shared with anyone. It was incredible! Later I realized how lucky I was to have had such an impressive and precise reading. I, of course, bought his book with my last $25 and went up to him later for his autograph. When he saw me he laughed and said, "You were so much fun to read for, you were so open."

I was open? He had a hot line to my mom from beyond, and he thought I was open! He absolutely knew which family members were here in body and who was there in spirit. He had started out by saying, "Betty, Bernadette, who is that?"

I replied, "It was my mother's sister."

"Your mother wants to send her love to her sister Betty."

How did he know she was still alive?

"Gosh, your parents travel with a crowd, Lou's here, Jack's here."

My parents travel with a crowd? I said nothing about my dad being deceased. Lou is my father's deceased brother, and Jack is my mother's brother who had passed several years before.

Then he said, "Who is Frank, Francis?

"I have a cousin we call Frank who's name is really Francis."

"Lou wants to send his love to Frank."

Lou was my father's brother and Frank's dad! How did he know that?

This was incredible. There were only two possible explanations: Mr. Van Praagh must have been at Thanksgiving dinner twenty years ago, or somehow my family was communicating from beyond. Since I had never even heard of James Van Praagh, let alone the fact that he was never at any family dinner, the latter must be true. Could this really be happening? I had one thousand witnesses.

It continued. "Rick, Richard, who is that?"

That is my daughter's father.

"Your mom wants you to know that he is a great man."

"Well," I said, "that's news to me." I didn't share that my mother wore black to our wedding and never said a nice word about the man, for good reason. He later proved himself to be physically abusive as well as a drug and alcohol addict. I was fortunate to come away from the marriage in one piece.

James was firm: "No, from your mother's new perspective, she can tell he is a great man. The reason you had challenges with him in this life was because he was beaten by his father as a small child."

This I knew was true. After I survived the first and only brutal attack, delivered in a drunken rage (I didn't hang around for more), I went to visit his aunt, his father's sister. She told me about her brother's abusive behavior toward his wife and children and his addiction to alcohol.

Successive therapists suggested that the abused often become the abuser. I took my daughter with his permission to California. Her safety was my priority, and distance seemed to be my only safety net. There is a happy ending to that story. The distance offered him the opportunity to become clean and sober. He later married an extraordinary woman and had three more children. Today, my daughter enjoys a close relationship, albeit still long distance, with her dad and his family.

James continued, "There are two identical necklaces with this exception—one has a white gold chain, the other yellow."

Right again, my daughter has my mother's heart necklace; I have mine, which my parents had made for me when I graduated high school. We put them on simultaneously the day after my mother passed, after shopping for new chains!

Then he said, "You are looking at two different properties." Up until then, I thought I was going to leave the marriage with what I came in with, so I had been house hunting. He continued, "One property has a very long concrete driveway, the other a large grassy yard. Your father says to get the concrete." Right again, perfect descriptions, and that would be just like my dad to say, "Go for less maintenance."

There was still more. "Your parents are buried in two separate places, divorce?"

"No," I said, "Italian."

They both wanted to be buried with their mothers. My father did not have the heart to make the decision and so, upon his passing, it was up to me. He had purchased four resting places—two where his parents are buried and two where my mother's parents are buried. Yes, I ended up with extra resting places. However, knowing well their wishes since childhood, the decision was easy. I placed each one accordingly. And although my parents are not lying side by side, I am sure I did well at following their wishes. Bottom line, I was at peace with it, the family a little uncomfortable, and James confused.

The last thing he said was the most unnerving. "Are you pregnant?" I shook my head no. I wanted to crawl into a hole. There I was in this room filled with hundreds of people, and he asked my most personal and painful question. I was going through my second devastating divorce at forty. Clearly my life dream to have another child was diminishing by the moment. He seemed not to notice my pain and said, "Your mother wants you to know that a baby boy is going to come through you." I was silent. I took the evening in and tried to process all that he had said over the days that followed. I couldn't imagine what was going to happen next.

# Chapter Nine -
# An Invitation from Out of the Blue

*"I will not wish thee riches, nor the glow of greatness, but that wherever*
*thou go some weary heart shall gladden at thy smile, or shadowed life*
*knows sunshine for a while. And so thy path shall be a track of light,*
*like angels' footsteps passing through the night."*
                    *—words on a church wall in Upwaltham, England*

I really do believe that we all live surrounded by Angels,
Angels who remind us that love never dies, it merely changes
form. Grief is a powerful emotion. It rides your heart, your mind,
and your soul like a roller coaster. Like the waves in the ocean,
sometimes you see them and sometimes they come up behind
you and crash you into the sand.

We only have power over how we choose to respond to any
given set of circumstances. I have moved through the pain that
occurs from those ghastly empty feelings of separation. Today, I
know that separation is an illusion.

What is real and what is illusion? It is a question I have been
asking myself since I was privileged to attend the last conference
that Shirley MacLaine created out in a Southern California desert.
I felt blessed because at only twenty-seven years old, I was witness
to a magnificent, healing light that came through a man named
Mauricio Panisset.

I received an invitation from out of the blue to attend a
conference hosted and created by a performer whom I had looked
up to in the dance scene my whole life. It was only weeks after my

birthday, and so it was my gift to me. I had just purchased a new white Jeep and so, with the top down, I made my way into the desert. When I arrived at a rugged retreat center near the Joshua Tree National Monument, I was assigned to a dorm filled with women who were clearly seekers, goddesses in their own right. After orientation, it was recommended we get to bed as soon as possible, as we would have an early start the next day.

There was a loud knock at our door at 4 am. Someone was inquiring to whom the white Jeep belonged. I sleepily realized that I was not going to get a parking ticket in the middle of cacti but rather be a volunteer to escort the music technician and Shirley's dear friend, former New York Congresswoman Bella Abzug, in my new four-wheel drive vehicle. Bella was a trailblazing feminist and passionate, relentless fighter for social and economic justice in this country and worldwide. I felt deeply honored to be able to have this woman in my front seat. She was awesome and a good sport about my driving.

The conference was more than I imagined it could be. We spent days in reflective conversations about the meaning of life. We meditated out in the desert morning and night and had the best vegetarian cuisine that I had ever tasted. This was an outstanding group of individuals who "coincidentally" had come together. Then we heard a rumor that Shirley had a surprise for us on the last night, a surprise that would change the way I looked at life forever.

Mauricio Panisset, a gifted Brazilian healer, had arrived with a translator. He was an older gentleman with a unique history, not particularly as pious as one would think from a person who bestows such miraculous gifts. As he stood before us, Shirley read his biography. There is now a wonderful book about his life, *Man of Light* by Kimberly Curcio.

He instructed those who felt they needed healing to come forward to the center of the room. He would start there. Then he would continue around the room. We were told he could see auras clearly and thereby know who was in need of a healing. Basically then it didn't really matter where you were sitting.

I chose to sit quietly in the back row. Several weeks earlier, I had carelessly injured my ankle falling off a curb while out for an early morning run. My ankle was still swollen; I had very little movement and was still limping to avoid putting too much weight on it. Now feeling my own skepticism, I decided to stay where I was so I could see in full view the music technician. I thought if any Hollywood special effects were present, he would be the man in control of them. To my surprise he sat awestruck as we watched light come from Mauricio's center and burst forth like a shower onto the receiver. It was a spectacular light show.

Now my moment had come. First Mauricio stood in front of me to heal the person directly ahead of me. Mauricio did not have a shirt on, and I saw a white light, similar to an electrical current appear like a road map, vibrating approximately an inch from the skin on his back. The fellow sitting next to me, wide-eyed, asked if I could see it too. I merely nodded my head. Then Mauricio walked behind me and, with loud guttural sound effects, he zapped me. I felt enveloped in this white, silvery light. I felt an electric shock wave through my center; my hands were glowing with this light for a moment and then the light was gone. Profound, amazing, unreal, I felt it all.

When he was done I walked outside in a daze, not realizing that I was no longer limping. I looked up at the stars shining so brilliantly and gazed in wonder. Growing up in New York, I had never had the opportunity to see the stars like this before. I walked across the desert to a gathering room where they were serving tea. I sat down and then, for the first time, looked at my ankle. The swelling was gone. I had full rotation; my ankle was completely healed! My imagination soared. What was the meaning for life and why are we here? Maybe it is not as complicated as we think. Perhaps we are just meant to be the light for one another.

*Angela Amoroso*

# Chapter Ten -
## Cadence the Rhythm of Light

*"Let your light shine. Shine within you so it can shine on someone else. Let your light shine!"*

—*Oprah Winfrey*

We have had the joy of watching my cousin and his girlfriend grow in their love for each other. We promised to always be there for them when they were married. I was thrilled to be at the birth of their first child, Cadence Paul Amoroso; being present to support those long hours, laboring a love so great, was my blessing.

Cadence was leaving Isabella's world and entering ours. He would be my messenger, in those moments right after his birth, as I held him for the first time. I spoke to his heart and asked him: What did she say? And his heart spoke to mine, "I love you, Mommy." It was our moment. It felt so real. And so five months later in New York we attended the christening of our godchild, Cadence Paul, the newest member of our family. My cousin took the picture—snap, there it was again, our precious, shining light.

It was pretty hilarious to see the faces on our New York relatives. It's OK when this kind of thing happens in California, but here on their New York turf? Isabella made her presence known, and as for Cadence Paul, my godson, he will always be my eternal messenger of love. Angels, we all live surrounded by Angels.

I have been asking big questions since I was a young teen, trying to understand just what sets the rhythm, the tempo, the pulse, and the pace; what is the cadence of life? What is our purpose? Why are we here? Why do terrible things happen? Why does the media seem so addicted to blame instead of promoting solutions? Why does violence sell? Why do drunk drivers live and innocent victims die? Why is there war? Why are there so many religious wars? Where was Jesus between the ages of twelve and thirty anyway? And why do babies die?

I asked my parents and my teachers. I asked the great philosophers, holy men and women. I questioned the scientists, doctors, and even businessmen. I asked those who seemed to be simple thinkers and those who had a flair for the complicated. I asked the homeless and rich. I asked the wealthy and the poor. I asked those who call themselves spiritual and those who call themselves religious. I asked all over the United States and in many countries. I read many books and still my questions went unanswered. I asked the musicians, and I listened to their music and their lyrics.

Still I remained frustrated. I felt as though something was missing. There was something that I was not getting—or was the information unavailable or grossly misgiven? I listened and heard all kinds of opinions. Yet, my cadence felt off. I couldn't understand how to get in the "flow" of life.

I was taught that God has given us a gift of free will, yet I was also taught that if you anger God by doing what is "displeasing," you will end up in the fires of hell. Depending what century and what particular brand of religion you are born into, or choose for that matter, the challenge of knowing for sure what pleases or displeases this God remains disputed even among today's respected authorities.

Albert Einstein said that all matter is energy vibrating at different frequencies. When I took my lifelong studies of science and religions and applied the teachings of Abraham, translated by Esther and Jerry Hicks, the cadence of my own understanding expanded and an overwhelming sense of peace came over me. It was then that Isabella appeared smack in the middle of her daddy's face. We searched back in photographs from when she first crossed over and found endless sightings.

Today my husband fancies himself as an orb hunter, photographing our friends in all sorts of places and time of day, using a variety of cameras. What are these beings of light? Are they the reflection of human souls before and after our physical experience here on this beautiful planet? This made me contemplate the words that Jesus the Christ said, "You are the Light of the World." In all the madness that has plagued humanity in the name of science and religion, would it not be profound that we find out, in our lifetime, that this particular quote is a literal translation that brings these two ambitious groups of science and religion together in peace and harmony?

My husband and I had the great pleasure of meeting with one of the greatest theologians of our time, Miceal Ledwith. When we brought him our Orb photos of Isabella and asked him my questions, he answered by asking me a question.

He said, "Do you know what Isabella means?"

"Of course," I said with confidence and pride. "It means dedicated to God."

He smiled and said, "Yes, I suppose you can say that, but the literal translation means 'Beautiful Jesus.'"

My life came full circle.

One of my favorite understandings from the Abraham teachings is that Life is about the "magnificent contrast." It is about matching our own vibration to the vibration that we want to experience. It's a match every time. I know that since I was in high school, I wanted to make a difference in people's lives and especially in the lives of children. I did not know in my youth what that would look like, and even now, each day another opportunity inspires greater vision.

I truly feel that my husband and I are in partnership with an angelic being we call Isabella. When I allow myself to feel the richness of the "magnificent contrast" and make my intention to move through the experience we call grief, I realize that I have learned on a very intimate level that there is no death, it is ALL GOOD. My husband reminds me, and I chuckle, about the great wisdom of Lucy, by Charles M. Schultz: "Good Grief, Charlie Brown!" Yes, Chuck knew it too. Even Grief is Good, and that, my dear friends, Is the Gift in Grief.

# Chapter Eleven -
# There Is a Blueprint, It Is a Healing TEAR

*"There can be no knowledge without emotion. We may be aware of a truth, yet until we have felt its force, it is not ours. To the cognition of the brain must be added the experience of the soul."*

*—Arnold Bennett*

My practice with grief has left me inspired to find the presence of God in all experiences. It has also shown me that there is no disaster plan for the unimaginable. Every experience is unique unto itself. There is nothing that can prepare us for the time when we experience the transition of a loved one. My own mother had endured over twenty years of Alzheimer's. When her time finally came, I thought I would be ready, even relieved. I was neither, and I began my bereavement process with more emotional waves of grief than I could have ever imagined.

Grief is a complicated, multidimensional, individual process that can never be generalized. Over time, brilliant minds have tried numerous ways to outline and explain it. The reality is that there is really no right or wrong way, no order of stages. There are no how-to's or shortcuts to move us through this passage of time. Yet, each of us in our own time will experience the journey and be forever changed.

I can only share my own experience of what supported me through those senseless moments that are now my blessing. In sharing my experience, it is my hope that you may find a blueprint to help you navigate your way around the pitfalls. It is my prayer that as you awaken on your journey, you will discover a new sense of peace.

Grief professionals often use the concept of "grief work" to help the bereaved through grief resolution. J. William Worden, in his book *Four Tasks of Mourning*, summarizes grief work by the acronym TEAR.

> *T = To accept the reality of the loss*
> *E = Experience the pain of the loss*
> *A = Adjust to the new environment without the lost object*
> *R = Reinvest in the new reality*

The shock that moves through our bodies at the moment we find our loved ones have passed is indescribable. The gift has been given. How we choose to unwrap the package, and begin to use it, is completely up to ourselves.

Initially, I have found that the body goes into automatic pilot, preparing for the memorial service, the burial, and all that goes into planning a well-deserved send off for our beloved. There can be all sorts of distractions, food deliveries, and visitors. Then in a relatively short time the community goes back to living their lives, and we are left alone. Grief becomes an uninvited flu that won't leave. I call it "the fog."

Days blend into each other, and now in retrospect I truly can't remember what happens after the funeral until the fog begins to lift. When does the fog lift? How can we move out from under this heaviness that seems to have the power to paralyze us at any moment? Awake or asleep there is no escape, no pause, and the desire to retreat forever can become frighteningly real.

Just before writing this chapter, I was standing in the lobby where I work when one of my students came rushing in screaming that her daddy had just died. Her mommy was behind her in a state of absolute shock. They had just parked the car when they received a call from three thousand miles away. There, her daddy had just finished the funeral for his own father, went for a casual run, and had a massive heart attack on the trail. I turned them around, drove them home, and stayed with them until their world, one by one, got the news and started showing up. In the time that I was alone with them, I will never forget that little girl's big blue eyes staring at me and asking, "How will we live?"

In all my own "grief work," I would have preferred to have lost Isabella over and over again, if it could have taken away the pain that I saw in her eyes. I merely said, "Together, one second at a time," and we cried and we cried and we cried, together.

Our American culture (diminished by the addictions to instant gratification and consumerism) is not well practiced with the patience and selflessness needed to support someone through their time of grieving. It is inevitable that maneuvering families through unchartered waters can be debilitating, as grief can magnify emotions. There is nothing like a wedding or a funeral to bring out the best and the worst in human beings.

We need to practice as a community how to be with someone who is grieving. If we can let go of our own insecurities and fears, we could learn to relax and just be there for each other. Not fix it. Not try and make it better—just be there and feel the loss together.

It never ceases to amaze me how people respond to someone who has just lost a loved one. They say things like, "I'm sorry," "How are you?" "Well, at least they lived a good long life," "You can have more children," "At least they didn't suffer," "Are you going to try again for another child?" and "Let me know if you need anything." Or even, "How can I help you?"

And the bereaved usually reply, "Fine," "I'm OK," "Thank you," and "I don't know."

When Isabella passed, my husband and I took a leave from work and stayed home together. He became my strength and I didn't want to be out of his company for a moment. The food deliveries were insurmountable, and we mused about how we could organize the masses to feed a small country. We watched sunsets and wrote songs and did whatever we could to start healing. In our desire to escape from the despair, we didn't even realize how far we were from the actual starting line.

Friends encouraged us to join support groups. The support groups had terrible negative names. I would remember a wise man once saying, "Don't join a group that has a name of something you don't want to be like." I couldn't see the point of a group so early on. My thought was that if I couldn't handle my own sadness, I was certainly too fragile to hear about someone else's pain. Theoretically knowing that there is great value in being part of a support group, we remained confident that the right opportunity would show itself at just the right time.

I often describe grief as an energy that needs to be diluted. It occurred to me that as a teacher I have seen parents of autistic children champion efforts for inclusion, the right for their child to be placed in the mainstream educational system. Intuitively, these fearless moms and dads know that their child will do better integrated rather than isolated with other autistic children. It could be something to ponder when we choose where to find our "support groups."

We live in San Diego and find our spiritual home in Los Angeles at The Agape International Spiritual Center. Just a month after Isabella's passing, we decided to commit to attending a ten-week class on prayer. Why? Well, when my husband went online to sign up, he had to click on a little twirling snowflake. That's right; on the Web site, when you signed up for the class, you had to click in the upper right hand corner on a rotating snowflake! How could we question the magic of this coincidence! This must be the right group, we thought.

The structure of the class was a two-hour lecture with a one-hour confidential discussion group. When we arrived, we requested that we be in the same group and described our current circumstance. I was clinging to my husband's arm, barely able to support myself, being out in public for the first time. The receptionist was sympathetic, yet when she put in our request to the powers that be, I remember the cold response, simply: if we were meant to be together we would be. A random drawing sent me across the room, seemingly out of the country, to sit with a group of strangers. I don't know what kept me from having some kind of dramatic emotional outburst. I awkwardly took my place in the circle and wrapped myself in a blanket, armed with my box of tissues.

Next we were assigned prayer partners that we would pray with at least once each week during the coming months. A late arrival joined our group, a five-month, exceedingly joyful, pregnant mommy. "Oh God," I remember thinking, "Please don't make this woman be my partner." What a cruel twist this would be. Totally random, we drew straws. The outcome: we ended up together. I used to often wonder, "How it is possible with six billion people on the planet that these kinds of coincidences can occur?" Not anymore! To make this example more stunning, can you guess what my new pregnant prayer partner did for a living? She was a hospice worker. Yes, God had provided me with my very own personalized grief expert to help me dilute my grief, and move through my pain. There is no doubt in my mind that the angel in her belly (I like to think a friend of Isabella's) brought her mommy to me with love.

In the throes of grief, isolation can be the leading cause of our suffering. Pain will pass, but we choose to suffer. Often the bereaved believes that no one else can imagine how we feel. And that is correct, because we are all unique and magnificent human beings. We will all find that we feel differently at any given moment faced with the dark side of loss. Finding the emotional support we need is yet another essential key that provides relief on the road to healing. Don't give up!

It is important to remember that we are not a well-versed society on death and dying. Some of our closest and most well-intentioned friends may say the wrong thing at the wrong time. It is important to be with others who have shared experiences. Don't underestimate the value of outside support. There are all kinds of support groups, therapists, professionals, self-help books, and more. Visit a variety of options until you find the right fit for you. You will know it when you get there. The Internet makes these kinds of searches easier than ever before. Ask friends for recommendations and follow through. Ask and it will come to you.

# Chapter Twelve - Weathering the Storm

*"To keep a lamp burning, we have to keep putting oil in it."*
—*Mother Teresa*

Moving through grief is like taking baby steps on the beach during a major hurricane. You really just want to run for cover, but grief yields and you must weather the storm, one small step at a time. It doesn't matter if the grief has entered your world suddenly or has been part of a long and agonizing chapter in your life. The weather has changed and there is no time to prepare. And many times no time to cook. So think raw!

Growing up Italian is like going to a university to get a degree in eating. Heavy cream sauces, gravies, red meat, lots of pasta and cheese were my daily staples. I have learned a lot about nutrition since my scrumptious childhood. More importantly, I have learned what works for me. May I pass the platter of inspiration to find what works for you. Nutrition is an essential place to start when you are grieving.

Our emotions respond to what we feed our bodies, both mentally and physically. If our blood sugars are imbalanced, it is unlikely that any psychologist, self-help book, or drug is going to make us feel better. So where do we begin? Who do we listen to? How do we know what is best for us to eat? There is a wonderful saying, "When the student is ready, the teacher will come." I am confident that you will find the answers you seek and that they will be uniquely your own. Here are some of the answers that I found worked for me.

It was not the way I thought life would look when I was turning forty. I was recently divorced, homeless (yes, homeless), and grieving the life I thought I lost. It was then that I bumped into a former student of mine, Daniel Schmachtenberger. This young man had participated in one of my productions as a young child. Nearly fifteen years later, he coincidentally stood before me and asked me how I was doing. "Not too well," was my reply, as if he couldn't tell by just looking at me. He asked if I would be willing to try something. I now had nothing to lose and said I would be willing to try anything. That day he became my teacher, and that moment will be forever yet another turning point in my life.

Daniel has a brilliant mind. He has an IQ that tops the charts, fascinating life experiences for someone so young, and an intuition that borderlines a modern mystic. He introduced me to what I now call hydrotherapy. It is a daily recommendation for an individual for the daily intake of water: one liter for every fifty pounds of weight. Additionally, when we sleep at night, all of the toxins settle in our organs. I leave a liter of water next to my bed when I go to sleep, and upon waking I drink my first liter of the day within fifteen minutes. This is a unique opportunity to flush the toxins from my system everyday.

To improve my digestion, I drink a liter of water thirty minutes before each meal and no liquid during meals. Then I wait two and a half hours after a meal and have another liter of water. It made sense to me that if we drink while we are eating, we dilute those valuable stomach acids that promote optimum digestion. Perhaps one of the best ways we can contribute to our health is by assisting our digestive system.

After talking to Daniel, I gave up caffeine, dairy, sugar, alcohol, and processed foods. I tried to eat as many raw vegetables as I could. Snacking on raw string beans was like having French fries. My rule of thumb was that if I couldn't imagine it in the

Garden of Eden then I didn't eat it. My vitamin supplement was Nature's First Food from www.rawfoods.com. This is a creative combination of land vegetables and algae. I'm sorry to disappoint any vegetarians out there, but I did have some broiled, organic chicken and wild Alaskan salmon from time to time. I had already given up red meat as a teenager. I found that I was rarely hungry and also found unexpected pleasures in desserts made from organic cottage cheese sweetened with Stevia and cinnamon.

I lost twelve pounds in my first month on this new food plan. After a week of suffering caffeine withdrawals (my former addiction had been two shots of espresso twice a day), I began to have more energy than ever before, even in the late afternoon! Before meeting Daniel again, I was certain that the stress in my life was destroying my immune system, and that I was probably only one diagnosis away from cancer. I changed my thoughts and my routine, and my life reflected those changes for the better.

I know the road that leads to a healthy body and mind includes a willingness to do whatever is necessary. Years later, I have kept my water regime as part of my daily routine. Do I have days when I don't meet my goals? Absolutely, and it is those times that I remember to practice being kind to myself and remember that my gift is the precious present.

On the trails of life, when I find grief as my companion, the need for exercise becomes an essential part of maintaining some degree of mental health and well-being. There is no secret out there regarding the value of exercise; getting motivated when your body aches from grief can seem even more challenging, especially if you do not have a regular routine already in place.

Grief can feel like the flu. It's hard to imagine ever feeling well again. Fortunately, all roller-coaster rides are temporary, even emotional ones! I start with baby steps, even if it means getting out and walking around the block for just five minutes. Taking the time for short intervals to breathe fresh air and stretch does wonders for relieving stress levels. Well-intentioned friends who have come to be a support or to lend a compassionate ear can easily walk with you instead of sitting indoors. Weather permitting, find yourself at the beach, a lake, or a neighborhood park, and allow nature to support you. Watch sunsets, birds, and squirrels. Don't be afraid to ask someone to bring you to a zoo, a museum, or an art exhibit.

If you already have an exercise program that you feel you can continue, just do it. Listen to your body and follow what it tells you. And, of course, always check with your physician before starting any new kind of exercise program. In time you may want to try a stretch class, a yoga class, or even a dance class! To start, think simple. A gentle daily walk can work wonders. It can even become something that you can begin to look forward to.

# Chapter Thirteen -
# To Love, to Serve, and to Remember

*"Life's most persistent and urgent question is, 'What are you doing for others?'"*

—*Martin Luther King, Jr.*

There is no right or wrong way to support a friend in need. Using our intuition and following our hearts is typically the best way to begin. The amazing Kanga Moms and their families are shining examples of what we as a human family can be for each other, creating traditions, remembering anniversaries for births and transitions, having grief parties, creating an art project, or planting something in the garden. Get creative and start having fun with it. The days of wearing black and beating our breasts in some kind of ritual lamentation can work for you if that's what you are looking for. But it is OK to feel happy again, and there is no timer that says you're done! Grief is over! To sustain your health is a lifelong process.

Just last year, as we were getting ready for Christmas, one of my dear friends' moms was making her final journey home. It had been a difficult time, and I offered to take one of her daughters, Mary, for the afternoon to bake cookies. No sooner than I arrived to pick her up, the call came. Mary had to go to her grandmother's house, so I went home to my husband. The family wanted their privacy, so I told Mary and her siblings that Drew and I would be praying for her grandma every fifteen minutes, so all they had to do was look at the clock and know that we were in prayer. Well, that's what came tumbling out of my mouth as I said good-bye to these children who would hold hands with grief that day and grow.

I had never promised to pray for someone so often, for so long—and soon Drew and I began to chant her grandma's name from wherever we were in the house. "Juuuuullllliaaaa," we would call out to each other, and her name became our prayer. For the next two days, as we prepared for our own family's holiday, Julia became ever-present with us. She inspired us to write for her a song that we recorded to bring tribute to a woman who lived with a zest for life found only on the stage!

For me, it was my husband who gently reminded me that our love came before Isabella. It was our love and grace that called her forth. It is this same love that will support us toward living a life that includes Isabella in a new way, a way that we could not have imagined before she transitioned!

Men and women grieve differently. We all move along the healing road at different paces. I know that I chose to be responsible for my emotions as much as I could. I held my ego accountable, and I took into consideration that I was not the only one missing Isabella. That may have given me the courage to be there for our family, too.

Just weeks after Isabella's passing, my daughter's boyfriend had planned a surprise engagement. After a romantic dinner and walk on the beach, they arrived at our home to share the wonderful news with us first. We would spend most of the New Year planning the wedding of her dreams. When they got back from their honeymoon, my daughter took me aside and thanked me for being able to have been present and make her feel so special in what must have been the most difficult time in my life.

We are all called to serve. All life has purpose. Life is abundant with opportunity to show up with the splendor that makes each of us as unique as snowflakes. Thoughts become Things! This is not a new idea. People have been thinking and creating all sorts of things since the beginning of humanity.

(Perhaps this is the meaning behind the Bible verse, "We are created in the image and likeness of God.")

Find out what speaks to you and go after it. No idea is too small or too big. Show up and help out an organization or start your own. There are no scorekeepers for who does more or less. Do what you feel comfortable with. But the key thing here is do something! There are plenty of organizations out there that need you now. At the very least, go visit an aging relative or neighbor, and bring a pizza with you.

Living three thousand miles away from loved ones is not easy, especially when life brings those challenges that come with aging family members. My godmother at ninety years young is the picture of health. Her younger sister, Connie, on the other hand, has had more than her share of sick days. One day, in the middle of the night, we received a call that Aunt Connie was in the hospital. My godmother, pleading for help, was more than we could bear: "Please come, I need you!" Well, there is nothing quite as sobering as hearing your ninety-year-old aunt asking for your help at 4 am. My husband jumped out of bed to make the travel arrangements, and we were on the next available flight.

They did not expect my aunt to live. Her kidneys were shutting down. We brought her pizza, thinking it could be her last meal, and sang her songs. Yet, before we knew it, Connie made a full recovery, and now a year later is still enjoying herself and the activities that surround her in a wonderful nursing home. Who knows what inspired her to stick around; maybe it was the pizza, or maybe it was just the love.

My two sweet aunts have spent their entire lives together. They were never married and have no children. My godmother visits Connie almost every day and the love is ever-present. We felt humbled and blessed to be able to jump on a plane and answer the call. When our plane landed at New York's John F. Kennedy Airport, a dragonfly bounced up and down on the wing of that plane in the morning sunlight. It felt as if my dad were saying, "So glad you could come!" Our visit didn't cure an old woman, who once again seemingly escaped the angel of death; we merely brought a little light to a dark corner. When we are willing to do our little part every day, our light glows brighter and that is all we have to do.

# Chapter Fourteen - I Will Be Your Light

*"There are two ways to live: you can live as if nothing is a miracle; you can live as if everything is a miracle."*

—*Albert Einstein*

Where is God? All relationships take time. Having a relationship with whatever you want to call the source intelligence that turns an acorn into an oak tree, every time, is up to you. For me, I know that as I practice more tolerance and compassion (with a knowing that love is not absent of discipline, respect, self responsibility, and universal laws, whether we choose to acknowledge them or not), I can learn to see and know the power of that source intelligence in all my experiences.

My mother used to tell me that God is everywhere. One day when I came home from a dance class, I accidentally placed my ballet slippers on the table. My mother became a little hysterical and threw them to the ground and told me never to put my shoes on the table because God is on the table. Well, if God is everywhere, then heaven isn't some place far beyond the stars; it is right here. Perhaps right here is in another dimension that, up until now, we couldn't see before.

And if God is right here, then our little Isabella is right here, and all of our loved ones who have transitioned before us are here too. And if that is true, you can imagine that I don't want to miss one miraculous moment of validation.

What earthly treasures can be more beautiful than those mysterious balls of light that show up in our photos? It is a new phenomena that is inspiring sensational and speculative discussions that ponder all kinds of amazing theories. For our family they have become a light for the world that reminds us that the kingdom of heaven is at hand.

We all can grow and practice emotional intelligence. It is possible to get comfortable with the mystery that is life and watch it enfold. For me it is even more exciting to know that we are on the cutting edge of comprehending information with more insight than ever before. We are matching vibrations of intelligent perception that has not been experienced in the history of humanity as we know it. When we catch the thought that we are responsible for creating our experience through the vibrational frequencies described by the great minds of our time, we can only conclude that we all have unlimited potential to meet the magnificent contrast of experience with confidence.

Grief provides an opportunity to leave us inspired to heal not only ourselves, but each other. My dance students chant the hit song from the Disney blockbuster hit, High School Musical, "We're all in this together!" It leaves me assured of how right they are!

I know it is easy to feel angry when I think of all the unrealized expectations. Isabella will never grace the stage as a baby snowflake. She will not enjoy our walks down to the beach to play in the sand and experience all the wonders that go along with growing up with mommy and daddy. After three months of enduring the intensive care unit, and all those unimaginable tests, tubes, and wires, to have only four days at home unplugged seems so very cruel.

Selfishly, we will never be able to fulfill our expectations as her parents, to hear her voice, or to know what it would have been like to take her to kindergarten and to be able to love her through all those experiential wonders that go along with growing up. I waited twenty-three years to have another baby, and to enjoy her for only ninety-six days seems to be less than fair.

And so we look for another perspective; this is only possible when we turn the other cheek. When we seek spiritual guidance, the answers are humbling. We will choose the path of eternal healing, for to identify with and become the pain rather than move through it would be to waste the sacrifice of this precious soul we call Isabella.

We wish to express our intention to make Isabella's premature birth and transition an opportunity to bring deeper meaning to all of our lives. May we all be transformed for the better by this tiny body with such a big message? God is all there is. God is Love and with God, All things are Possible. So Dream Bigger, Love Unconditionally, Do More, and get out there and Live on Purpose.

Angels. We all live surrounded by Angels. We watch sunsets from our window and Drew says, "Look, Isabella has her paints out again." The sky is a brilliant orange just like our giraffe friends. We choose to dwell in a deep knowing that Isabella lived and fulfilled her own expectations with grace and purpose. Blessed are we to have been able to assist our daughter in her life mission for unity and love. The creation of Isabella's Giraffe Club is only the beginning for our own premature birth into our unknown future.

The secret of life? There is no secret. We are here to love, to serve, and to be the light. May your journey be filled with the light where all love resides and may you notice a coincidence every day to help you remember who you really are.

# Bibliography

Arlin, Stephen. Raw Power. San Diego: Maul Brothers Publishing, 2002. (www.rawfoods.com)

Barrett, Greg, and Jane Hopkins. Wailana the Waterbug. Honolulu: Mutual Publishing, 1999.

Beckwith, Michael Bernard. Inspirations of the Heart. Culver City, Calif.: Agape Global Ventures, 2004.

Blanchard, Ken, and Phil Hodges. Lead Like Jesus. Nashville: Thomas Nelson, 2005.

Dyer, Wayne. Inspiration. Carlsbad, Calif.: Hay House, 2006.

Chapman, Gary, and Dr. Ross Campbell, M.D. The Five Languages of Children. Chicago: Northfield Publishing, 1997.

Chopra, Deepak. The 7 Laws of Spiritual Success. Co-published by Amber-Allen Publishing and New World Library, 1994. (www.chopra.com)

Curcio, Kimerly. Man of Light, Mauricio Panisset. New York: Select Books, 2002.

Eberle, Gary. Dangerous Words. Boston: Trumpeter, 2007.

Foo, Wei Zhong. Da Dao Chan Gong. Ft. Lauderdale: Da Dao Chan Gong Center, 2002.

Goleman, Daniel. Emotional Intelligence. New York: Bantam Books, 1995.

Hanh, Thich Nhat. Touching Peace. Berkeley: Parallax Press, 1992.

Hay, Louise L. You Can Heal Your Life. Carlsbad, Calif.: Hay House, 1999.

Hicks, Esther and Jerry. Ask and It Is Given (The Teachings of Abraham). Carlsbad, Calif.: Hay House, 2004.

Hoe, Susan Ludington. Kangaroo Care. New York: Bantam Books, 1993.

Holmes, Ernest. Living the Science of Mind. Camarillo, Calif.: DeVorss Publications, 1984.

Jensen, Dr. Bernard. Foods That Heal. New York: Avery, 1988.

Johnson, Spencer. The Precious Present. New York: Doubleday, 1981.

Kornfield, Jack. A Path with Heart. New York: Bantam Books, 1993.

Ledwith, Miceal, and Klaus Heinemann. The Orb Project. New York: Beyond Words, 2007.

MacLaine, Shirley. The Camino. New York: Pocket Books, 2000.

Mongan, M., and Marie F. Hy. HypnoBirthing: A Celebration of Life. Concord, N.H.: Rivertree Publishing, 1992.

Nelson, Jane. Positive Discipline for Teenagers. Rocklin, Calif.: Prima Publishing, 1994.

Noel, Brook, and Pamela D. Blair. I Wasn't Ready to Say Goodbye. Milwaukee: Champion Press, 2000.

Linden, Dana Wechsler, Emma Trenti Paroli, and Mia Wechsler Doron, M.D. Preemies. New York: Pocket Books, 2000.

Orman, Suze. Suze Orman's Financial Guidebook. New York: Three Rivers Press, 1998.

Peck, Scott M. The Friendly Snowflake. New York: Barnes & Noble, 1992.

Redfield, James. The Celestine Prophecy. New York: Warner Books, 1993.

Robertson, Jon and Robin. The Sacred Kitchen. Novato, Calif.: New World Library, 1999.

Robbins, John. May All Be Fed, Diet for a New World. New York: Avon Books, 1992.

Ruiz, Don Miguel. The Four Agreements. San Rafael, Calif.: Amber-Allen Publishing, 2001.

Teilhard de Chardin. The Phenomenon of Man. New York: Harper & Row, 1965.

Tharp, Twyla. The Creative Habit. New York: Simon & Schuster, 2006.

Ullman, Robert, and Judyth Reichenberg-Ullman. Mystics, Masters, Saints and Sages. Boston: Canari Press, 2004.

Walsch, Neale Donald. The Little Soul and the Sun. Charlottesville: Hampton Roads Publishing, 1998.

Rushnell, Squire. When God Winks. New York: Atria Books, 2002.

Wolfe, David. Eating for Beauty. San Diego: Maul Brothers Publishing, 2002.

Worden, William. J. Four Tasks of Mourning. Adapted from Grief Counseling and Grief Therapy: A Handbook for the Mental Health Practitioner. New York: Springer Publishing, 1982.

Williamson, Marianne. The Healing of America. New York: Simon & Schuster, 1997.

Zukav, Gary. The Dancing Wu Li Masters. New York: HarperCollins, 1979.

# Resources

**Agape International Spiritual Center**
Rev. Dr. Michael Bernard Beckwith
5700 Buckingham Parkway
Culver City, CA 90230
(310) 348-1250
www.AgapeLive.com

**Seaside Center for Spiritual Living**
Dr. Rev. Christian Sorensen
1613 Lake Drive
Encinitas, CA 92024
(760) 753-5786
www.SeasideChurch.org

**The Unity Center**
Rev. Wendy Craig-Purcell
8999 Activity Road
San Diego, CA 92126
(858) 689-6500
www.TheUnityCenter.net

**Optimum Health Institute**
6970 Central Avenue
Lemon Grove, CA 91949
(800) 843-0165
www.optimumhealth.org

**Compassionate Communication Workshops**
Kelly Bryson M.A., MFT,
3614 Porter Gulch Rd.
Aptos, CA 95003
(831) 462-3277(EARS)
(877) 663-3277 (NO-FEARS)
E-mail: kelly@LanguageOfCompassion.com

Karl and Jeanne Anthony
www.KarlAnthony.com
(800) 993-0165

Daniel Schmachtenberger
www.experiencethesource.com

James Van Praagh
www.vanpraagh.com

March of Dimes
www.marchofdimes.com

First Candle
www.sidsalliance.org
(800) 221-7437

Alzheimer's Association
www.alz.org

Rachelle Joy Benveniste
Writer-Poet-Writing Coach
rachellejoyb@gmail.com
310-398-9316

Printed in the United States
125701LV00004B/1/P

9 780595 488339